PRAISE FOR RIGHTEOUS AND LOS

"Stuck in a spiritual rut? Striving for closeness with God, yet feeling like he's further away than ever? Take a seat with Michelle as she shares her secret to closeness with God. Allow her to pour a tall, cool glass of refreshing truth, taking you straight to the arms of Jesus. For anyone out there who knows there's something more, but can't seem to find it, this book is for you!"

—**Erica Wiggenhorn,** author of *An Unexplainable Life: Recovering the Wonder & Devotion of the Early Church* and *The Unexplainable Church: Reigniting the Mission of the Early Believers*

"With her scriptural insights and life experiences, Michelle leads you to a deeper understanding of the parable of the prodigal son—especially the feelings of his older brother. She personally relates to those feelings, and you will too as she challenges your thinking through end-of-chapter discussion questions. Her research enriches the book with snippets from the writings of others. You will surely recognize some flawed attitudes of your own as you ponder her points."

—**Shirley Brosius,** speaker and author of *Sisterhood of Faith: 365 Life-Changing Stories about Women Who Made A Difference*

"I identify with the 'older brother,' so I appreciate Michelle Lazurek's gentle wisdom. Her vulnerable sharing assures us God is wooing us into sweet intimacy with a loving, welcoming Father who does not condemn. This significant book helps us see the subtle elder brother responses we can easily ignore. Yet it offers even more hope for freedom-producing healing. Even if you don't think you are like the older brother, read this book—you will benefit."

—**Kathy Collard Miller,** speaker and author of many books, including *Never Ever Be the Same: A New You Starts Today*

Righteous & Lost

Righteous & Lost

Finding Hope for the Pharisee Within

MICHELLE S. LAZUREK

LEAFWOOD
PUBLISHERS
an imprint of Abilene Christian University Press

RIGHTEOUS AND LOST

Finding Hope for the Pharisee Within

LEAFWOOD PUBLISHERS
an imprint of Abilene Christian University Press

ISBN 978-0-89112-436-8

Printed in the United States of America

Published in association with WordWise Media Services, 4083 Avenue L, Suite 255, Lancaster, CA 93536.

Cataloguing in Publication data available through the Library of Congress.

Cover design by ThinkPen Design, LLC | Interior text design by Sandy Armstrong, Strong Design

Leafwood Publishers is an imprint of Abilene Christian University Press
ACU Box 29138, Abilene, Texas 79699

1-877-816-4455 | www.leafwoodpublishers.com

17 18 19 20 21 22 / 7 6 5 4 3 2 1

To my fellow Pharisees
Come out from the field and into the Party

Acknowledgments

As someone who has served in churches for over twenty years, I know what it is like to go through the motions of faith. I myself have come into church grumbling under my breath as I go through the routine of worship and serving in various capacities. To all the churches I have ever been a part of, thanks for letting me work to tend God's fields even in the moments when I didn't see what a joy it was to be in God's presence. Thanks for loving me and inviting me to the feast anyway.

To my loving husband, Joe, and to my children, Caleb and Leah, thanks for your patience and forbearance, even when the grumbling got louder than just under my breath.

To my agent, advocate, and friend, Steve Hutson, thanks for advocating for this book to get into print. You may never see the fruit your work has yielded in the field, but God does. One day, we will toast your accomplishments at the party too.

To the team at Leafwood Publishers, especially Gary Myers, thank you for seeing the worth not only in my work as a writer but in the rejuvenating work the Holy Spirit will do in the lives of the lost members of the body of Christ because of its existence. We will have much to celebrate when we meet again, Gary.

Contents

Introduction

We all know the story. Jesus tells the tax collectors and sinners a story about a father who has two sons. The younger son asks for his inheritance early, and when he gets it, he proceeds to squander it on loose and wild living until he is destitute, forced to live in a pig farm with nothing to eat but leftover garbage. Once he hits rock bottom, he sheepishly approaches his father, who lovingly embraces him and hosts a lavish feast celebrating his son.

Perhaps this story has spoken to you during some difficult times in your life. Maybe you have made some bad decisions in your life and have engaged in sinful practices that have cost you, like the prodigal son, your wealth, resources, and, most importantly, those you love. Maybe you have read this parable and opened your eyes to God's unconditional love that, if you are willing, he is waiting to lavish on you. Perhaps you have run into God's arms, saying, "Father, I have sinned against you and against heaven. I am no longer worthy to be called your son or daughter." Maybe you have felt the warm embrace of the Father, assuring you that everything you have ever done or ever will do is covered under his Son's blood. This story carries great hope for all those who read it.

But then there's the part that you may have missed. It's the part Jesus chooses to leave until the end, an obvious lesson to the snickering Pharisees, who, among the tax collectors, thumb their noses at his insinuation. He adds a few words about the *other* brother, the one Jesus chooses not to name; the one grumbling under his breath about the music he hears in the distance. The music he never got to dance to, the fatted calf he never ate, the love he thinks he never received.

This sibling rivalry is nothing new. Yet this is more than mere rivalry. It's a silent war that rages within the elder brother, a force that drives a wedge not only between him and his brother, but also between him and his father, a wedge that keeps him from receiving his father's love. The prodigal son parable is more than just a story; it's a parallel between those that realize their lostness and repent, and those that never realize they are lost at all. The ones who don't know they are lost are the people who put a fake plastic smile on their faces and with perfectly coiffed hair and neatly pressed shirts, waltz through the church's doors every Sunday and take their rightful position at their regular pew and pretend nothing is wrong. When all the while the enemy chews away at their soul, like a cancer gone undiagnosed: subtle at first, then it embeds itself into the core of their being. Every jeer, every scoff puts them back on that field, as distant as they can be from the father, slaving away at work, hoping that every gesture of sacrifice might bring them closer to the wedding feast.

I know this because it's me.

The sad part is, most churches are full of people like me.

It took me a long time to realize that my father has been pleading with me, too, wanting me to celebrate with him. Yet I was so busy slaving away at church programs and "doing church" that I had forgotten the reason why I was doing it in the first place.

Before I knew it, I was so far off in the distance that I had to come closer just to hear the music. My father waited at the door for me, extending a hand and escorting me into the party, a party held in my honor.

There's a party being held for you, too. The question is: Will you come in from the field to attend?

This book is for the Pharisee, the other brother, the one working hard at doing and being right.

Will you be my guest?

Chapter One

The True Meaning of Lostness

Attending church as I normally did one Sunday, I sat in my same seat, greeted the same people, and went through the normal Sunday morning routine. Listening to my husband preach that morning, he challenged the congregation to come up for prayer if they wanted more of God. A few people went up to the front of the altar, and many people surrounded them in prayer as they prayed that the Holy Spirit would pour himself out on his people.

That morning, I came to a startling realization: I didn't want more.

In fact, I couldn't remember the last time I wanted more of God. How could a pastor's wife be stuck spiritually? I attended church weekly, occasionally opened my Bible, and prayed whenever I wanted something that was important to me. I was surviving, but I wasn't thriving. In short, I was stuck. Like a set of tires spinning wildly, I was hopelessly trying to achieve intimacy with God but getting nowhere.

Maybe you feel like I felt that day. Maybe you crack open your Bible, point to a random verse, and start reading, hoping the Lord will speak to you after months (or maybe even years) of silence. Perhaps you feel utterly alone, hopeless that you will ever have that intimate connection you so desperately seek.

But there's hope. If you've ever felt like something was missing in your life, you are not alone.

Reading my Bible one day, I reread the book of Genesis, and I saw Genesis 1:2 in a new light. "Now the earth was formless and empty, darkness was over the surface of the deep, and the Spirit of God was hovering over the waters." God created the heavens and the earth. But he knew something was missing. Since the beginning of time, the earth as we know it has had a void, an emptiness that only God can fill. God has been trying to fill the void in our lives ever since. God's intention, even in paradise, is for us to never feel that void. He wants us to fill it with the joy that comes from fellowship with him rather than remain (like the earth) formless and empty. He hovers over us, too, waiting to allow his people to drink from the waters that flow from that fellowship.

God wanted fellowship with me too. However, I often replaced time *with* him with doing stuff *for* him. This kept my spiritually starved soul craving more. That morning at church, though, I had had enough. I wanted to trade my spiritually artificial life for one of authentic, abundant living. Like the woman at the well in John 4, I wanted a sip from God's well, one overflowing with living, thirst-quenching water. I stepped up to the altar, arms outstretched to the heavens, begging God to meet with me.

And he did.

With a soft touch on the back of the shoulder from a fellow congregation member, I felt a sudden peace overwhelm me like never before. I prayed that the Holy Spirit would enter my heart anew, and all of the hopelessness and emptiness that I had been feeling instantly disappeared. God was hovering over me like he was hovering over the waters that first day in the Genesis account, waiting for me to fellowship with him. A simple prayer and acknowledgment of my spiritual depravity was all it took to renew my relationship with God. It happened to me, and it can happen to you too. When I went home, I felt different. No more anger. No more sadness. Just hope.

I just wanted God to meet me where I was and fill that deep, aching void that can only be filled through relationship with him, and he did. But so many of us go through the motions of faith, attending church service after church service, soaking in every sermon, doing nothing with them. Just like the brothers depicted in the parable of the prodigal son, churches are filled with people like me whose highlight of the day is checking off church on their to-do list. But what they don't know is that they are wanderers. This is not what God intended for them.

If you are not familiar with the passage, let me repeat it for you here:

> There was a man who had two sons. The younger one said to his father, "Father, give me my share of the estate." So he divided his property between them. Not long after that, the younger son got together all he had, set off for a distant country and there squandered his wealth in wild living. After he had spent everything, there was a severe famine in that whole country, and he began to be in need. So he went and hired himself out to a citizen of that

country, who sent him to his fields to feed pigs. He longed to fill his stomach with the pods that the pigs were eating, but no one gave him anything.

When he came to his senses, he said, "How many of my father's hired servants have food to spare, and here I am starving to death! I will set out and go back to my father and say to him: Father, I have sinned against heaven and against you. I am no longer worthy to be called your son; make me like one of your hired servants." So he got up and went to his father.

But while he was still a long way off, his father saw him and was filled with compassion for him; he ran to his son, threw his arms around him and kissed him.

The son said to him, "Father, I have sinned against heaven and against you. I am no longer worthy to be called your son."

But the father said to his servants, "Quick! Bring the best robe and put it on him. Put a ring on his finger and sandals on his feet. Bring the fattened calf and kill it. Let's have a feast and celebrate. For this son of mine was dead and is alive again; he was lost and is found." So they began to celebrate.

Meanwhile, the older son was in the field. When he came near the house, he heard music and dancing. So he called one of the servants and asked him what was going on. "Your brother has come," he replied, "and your father has killed the fattened calf because he has him back safe and sound."

The older brother became angry and refused to go in. So his father went out and pleaded with him. But he answered his father, "Look! All these years I've been

> slaving for you and never disobeyed your orders. Yet you never gave me even a young goat so I could celebrate with my friends. But when this son of yours who has squandered your property with prostitutes comes home, you kill the fattened calf for him!"
>
> "My son," the father said, "you are always with me, and everything I have is yours. But we had to celebrate and be glad, because this brother of yours was dead and is alive again; he was lost and is found." (Luke 15:11–32)

It's obvious from this story that Jesus is pinpointing the Pharisees in the depiction of the brother. But Jesus's will is even for the Pharisee like me to receive the salvation available from the Father.

I wish I could say the above scenario is only one situation among many happy years of being a pastor's wife. Yes, there have been many special moments I have shared as a pastor's wife that have been the highlight of my life as a Christian. But if I'm honest, there have been many ordinary moments, the special days drowning in the mundane ones, and it has been enough to make me want to quit. These days were ones when God and life didn't quite make sense. I've read the Bible cover to cover a few times, and each page drips with the miraculous inner workings of a God who is close to his people, even when they are not close to him. It started with Adam and Eve, and continues today, the beloved desperately drinking from the well that they hope will give them the living water they long for. As Christians, we may not drown our sorrows at the bottom of a bottle of beer, but we self-medicate in other ways. The panacea comes in the form of the second piece of pie after dinner or that prayer request covered in gossip at the prayer meeting. We don't realize we are living apart from God, but we are. With every whisper behind my friend's back or every gulp of diet soda, I'm tearing myself away from the vine that gives me life. I get a rise out of tearing others down so I can build myself up, another panacea that allows me to wander even further from the father.

A few years ago, I acted like the older brother, too. For the first few years of my working life after I got married, God called me to become a daycare/preschool teacher. If you've never thanked your child's teacher for all they do, do it! It may seem like a glamorous position, working around the limited school calendar, giving the class every excuse to have a party or watch a movie, but they do so much to teach your child in the formative years of life. They not only teach the basics of education, but they are also the main holders of the building blocks that form their character, emotional and mental health, and build a strong self-concept. Not only was I in charge of all this, but as a Christian, I also wanted to form their spiritual development. This, along with children struggling with social and emotional challenges, makes for some long, draining days. I knew God was calling me to something more; I just wasn't sure what it was. With limited time and an even more limited bank account, I had no choice but to work to support our household while my husband did his best to grow a church plant and work a second job to supplement our income as well. Every day on my lunch break, I'd beg God to give me a job that would utilize my leadership abilities and that would be a job that I loved. Eventually, we had to close down the church plant and move to take another position within our denomination. This freed me to focus full-time on my writing. I have never been so fulfilled in my career. But those years before the move taxed me physically, emotionally, financially, and spiritually. I was slipping further away from God, making myself miserable. I was so mad at God for putting me in that position, I thought I'd never get over it.

Perhaps that's where the older brother got stuck, too. Maybe, like me, he got tired of going through the motions of life. It's obvious from the story that the father loved both sons equally, but it's evident the older brother didn't believe that. Maybe he wanted more out of life than working for his father. It was customary during that culture for the father to pass on the family business to his sons, particularly the oldest son. It would have been a thrill to carry on the traditions of the generation before him. But something sends him out into the field "to slave." Doesn't sound like much of an honor, does it? Perhaps he's jealous of the younger brother's freedom, nothing holding him back or tying him down to the family. His brother had a taste for something more, a chance for his heart to run wild. The older brother also had a taste for something more: the love and approval of a father he thought he didn't have. Both had misplaced values and priorities, yet one gets a party thrown in his honor. Why?

This is a question the older brother must have asked himself. I can imagine him walking away, scoffing, *Why does he get all of Dad's love and approval? He doesn't even deserve it! Here I am doing all the work, and he's not even lifting a finger to help!* Sound familiar?

> As Jesus and his disciples were on their way, he came to a village where a woman named Martha opened her home to him. She had a sister called Mary, who sat at the Lord's feet listening to what he said. But Martha was distracted by all the preparations that had to be made. She came to him and asked, "Lord, don't you care that my sister has left me to do the work by myself? Tell her to help me!"
>
> "Martha, Martha," the Lord answered, "you are worried and upset about many things, but few things are needed—or indeed only one. Mary has chosen

> what is better, and it will not be taken away from her."
> (Luke 10:38–42)

This isn't the first time we've seen older siblings get so bogged down in the distractions of work that they forget to focus on the "better thing." Instead of reveling in the blessing of being a good steward of the family's possessions, they got caught up in the trap of comparison, their love for their family giving way to a secret fire brewing in their souls.

Tim Keller, author of *Prodigal God,* said,

> It is natural for younger brothers to think that elder brotherness and Christianity are exactly the same thing. But Jesus says they are not. In his parable, Jesus deconstructs the religiosity that is one of the main problems with the world. In this parable Jesus says to us, "Would you please be open to the possibility that the gospel, real Christianity, is something very different from religion?" That gives many people hope that there is a way to know God that doesn't lead to the pathologies of moralism and religiosity.[1]

The true meaning of lostness is trading relationship for religion, grace for works, freedom for bondage. Both sons were lost. But only one of them realized it.

This book is to let the present-day Pharisees realize it and wander back to the feast.

DISCUSSION QUESTIONS

1 Which son have you related to as you have read the Parable of the Lost Son? Has that perspective changed after reading this chapter?

2 "The true meaning of lostness is trading relationship for religion, grace for works, freedom for bondage. Both sons were lost. But only one of them realized it." Have you ever felt this way? Have you ever thought of being lost in this context before?

3 Have you ever replaced time with God with doing things for God? How do you think this contributes to someone's lostness in his/her spiritual journey?

NOTE

[1]Tim Keller, *The Prodigal God: Recovering the Heart of the Christian Faith* (New York: Riverhead Books, 2008), 69–70.

Chapter Two

Who Is the Eldest Brother?

I've listened to many sermons on this parable. Every sermon has focused on the prodigal son, the rebellious ingrate who ran away from the blessings he already had to pursue a wild and ultimately fruitless lifestyle. All those sermons left the eldest out in the field, brooding and envious over all the prodigal got instead of what he got. Frankly, we see him as self-righteous, selfish, and jealous.

But is that all he is, or is he something more?

Think for a moment about some of the other people in the Bible who seem to get a bad reputation. We have Martha, who was more worried about her work than her worship. Peter, who spoke too quickly and who denied vehemently. Paul, whose zeal for the wrong thing actually turned him into a warrior for the right thing when guided by the Holy Spirit. David, named a man after God's own heart, who was also an adulterer and a murderer. Sounds like the Bible is full of unsavory characters!

Consider for a moment what the Bible would be like without them: Martha, gently chastised by Christ for not choosing "the better thing," doesn't seem to let even her friend's words deter her from her work or from a future relationship. John 11:5 says,"Now Jesus loved Martha and her sister and Lazarus." Jesus loved Martha, even when he knew she was easily distracted by other things. Also, Mary, the one that Jesus praised for her ability to worship, is now named "the other sister." Despite Martha's inability to put aside the idol of work, without her, what would Jesus and the numerous other people coming to the house have to eat? Would they eat with their hands, or would they use the dishes Martha had set on the table? Furthermore, in John 11 we get a glimpse of a special moment between Martha and Jesus. After her brother Lazarus died, Martha follows Jesus out to the field because she wants answers, and she's not leaving without them. Jesus must have respected the faith she displayed when she came to him demanding an answer to why he didn't come to save her brother:

"When Martha heard that Jesus was coming, she went out to meet him, but Mary stayed at home. 'Lord,' Martha said to Jesus, 'if you had been here, my brother would not have died. But I know that even now God will give you whatever you ask'" (John 11:20–22). There is this change that has taken place in Martha from their first exchange in her home. His words seem to have changed her enough to make meeting Jesus her first priority. Jesus has a place in his kingdom for both types of people: the sheep that he has to go call back into the fold as well as the ninety-nine who follow closely in place behind the shepherd.

Concerning David, 1 Samuel has telling words regarding God and his choice of people. "But the Lord said to Samuel, 'Do not consider his appearance or his height, for I have rejected him. The Lord does not look at the things people look at. People look at the outward appearance, but the LORD looks at the heart'" (16:7). Even when God foreknew David's actions with Bathsheba, he still chose him as a ruler for the people because his heart at one time was in the right place.

God has a place in the kingdom for the screw-ups, the rebellious, wandering hearted, and also for the rule-follower, with neatly pressed pants with newly ironed pleats. Singer and songwriter Carolyn Arends, in her article titled "The Other Prodigal Son," said, "When we considered the fact that Jesus told this story to the Pharisees (older brothers if ever there were some!) in response to their outrage over his association with 'sinners,' we realized the parable is *primarily* about the father's relationship with the older son."[1]

The eldest is the star of this parable? Perhaps it is just as important to understand that there is room in the kingdom for both these men, and that both brothers were lost, and grace and hope were still available to them both.

WHO ARE THE PHARISEES?

Researching this subject, one website stated,

> [The Pharisees] were mostly middle-class businessmen, and therefore were in contact with the common man. The Pharisees were held in much higher esteem by the common man than the Sadducees. Though they were a minority in the Sanhedrin and held a minority number of positions as priests, they seemed to control the decision making of the Sanhedrin far more than the Sadducees did, again because they had the support of the people. Religiously, they accepted the written Word as inspired by God. . . . In contrast to the Sadducees, they believed the following:

1. They believed that God controlled all things, yet decisions made by individuals also contributed to the course of a person's life.
2. They believed in the resurrection of the dead.
3. They believed in an afterlife, with appropriate reward and punishment on an individual basis.
4. They believed in the existence of angels and demons.

> Though the Pharisees were rivals of the Sadducees, they managed to set aside their differences on one occasion—the trial of Christ. It was at this point that the Sadducees and Pharisees united to put Christ to death.[2]

That doesn't sound so bad, right? It wasn't, until they began to think that traditions had the same authority as God's Word and held the people to a rigid set of rules that, if not observed, resulted in punishment. Reggie McNeal, author of *This Present Future,* says,

> The disciples had grown up under the influence of Pharisaic Judaism. The Pharisees' evangelism strategy sounds eerily familiar. Their approach to sharing God was, "Come and get it!" In addition, they had contorted God's message to moralism: "You people out there need to straighten up!" The Pharisees had developed an insular culture. . . . Their message to people outside the bubble was: "Become like us (translated: believe like us, dress like us, vote like us, act like us, like what we like, don't like what we don't like). If you become like us (jump through cultural hoops and adopt ours), we will consider you for club membership."[3]

Ouch! This is sounding more and more like me after all. This sounds a lot like the eldest brother in the parable as well. When his father didn't conform to the "rules" the eldest had in his mind that he should follow (including those of society), he got angry. His father certainly wasn't acting the way a father should. So, he must be wrong, right? But what the eldest forgot about was grace. Grace is the nemesis of Pharisaic thinking. If the eldest was the symbol of the Pharisees, was Jesus the father in the parable or someone else?

Jesus: The Original Older Brother

It is obvious through the prodigal son parable that an invitation to the feast was offered to both the eldest and the prodigal. The parable makes it seem as if the prodigal is the better of the two sons: repentant, forgiving, humbled. The eldest seems ornery, full of complaints and unwilling to repent. But Jesus has grace for both sons, because Jesus understands the sins of both—the one who recognizes his sin and saves himself before it is too late, and the other son who thinks he is doing fine and never bothers to do the soul-searching necessary for wholeness. He understands this because he is an older brother. In an article published in *Journal for Preachers*, Theodore Wardlaw writes,

> The real issue, theologically speaking—the issue that just rubs them raw—is that, all across the pages of the Gospels, he leaves them outside in the cold and goes in himself to join in the festive party. He's supposed to be all the time drawing and reinforcing lines in the world, and instead he's forever stepping over them in the name of a God who so loved us that God gave the ultimate older brother to put his arms around every prodigal in the world.
>
> So how dare we dismiss the older brother here in this text! He's more than we make of him. For he, too, knows

> more than he's letting on about the sustaining grace and mercy of God.[4]

What a beautiful analogy! If the father was such a bad guy, why did the eldest remain to take care of his father's property? He'd already seen his brother walk away, forsaking his obligations. Why not him, too? Perhaps he knows more about the grace and mercy of his father than what we glean from this story. In a sense, Jesus is the older brother, dying for the world and for all of God's children. Since he existed before time, he is our older brother, and as older brothers (and the eldest) demonstrate, they make more sacrifices than is required of them so that all the younger brothers and sisters can have the best life possible.

THE PARTY

Middle Eastern culture valued the gift of celebration, often hosting lavish parties to celebrate special events and the people in their lives. Blogger Casey Groff said,

> In general, partying is a way to celebrate something in community or even just to have fun for no real reason at all. How much more should you, as a Christian, live every day celebrating because you have the best reason of all to celebrate—God's unconditional love for you! . . . As a Christian, you are to be marked by supernatural joy and spirits of celebration, embracing each day as a party for Jesus.
>
> So why again is this important? It's not about going to parties and abstaining from everything while sitting in the corner with your arms crossed, judging everyone else; this in no way embodies the love of Christ for the lost. In fact, nothing about that posture will create any space for others to know Jesus. But someone in the same

> circumstances who is filled with the celebratory spirit Jesus desires can truly share Jesus in an authentic and powerful way.[5]

Instead of sitting with his arms crossed, the eldest doesn't go in at all. The eldest son's envy reigns supreme again as he refuses to go into the party celebrating his brother's change of heart. Yet his heart must be broken, too. But why is his heart broken? Is it because his brother walked away from him, rejecting him and their relationship? The bigger question to ask ourselves as we read this story is not why does he not go into the party, but why would the prodigal leave his brother in the first place? I can imagine what the eldest felt when the prodigal left that day. Did the eldest look on in sorrow as he watched his brother walk away from everything, including him? The relationship between the eldest and the prodigal must have been strained from the beginning. If the prodigal's relationship with the eldest was so great, why would he run off to find his worth and value in strangers rather than from his family?

But this is nothing new. Sibling rivalry has been an issue since after the fall. Adam and Eve had issues right after the taste of that shiny red apple hit Eve's lips:

> And he said, "Who told you that you were naked? Have you eaten from the tree that I commanded you not to eat from?"
>
> The man said, "The woman you put here with me—she gave me some fruit from the tree, and I ate it."
>
> Then the LORD God said to the woman, "What is this you have done?"
>
> The woman said, "The serpent deceived me, and I ate." (Gen. 3:11–13)

Adam and Eve's sin paved the way for a whole new generation of sinners, starting with Cain and Abel. Cain killed Abel the second he didn't like something he had done:

> The LORD looked with favor on Abel and his offering, but on Cain and his offering he did not look with favor. So Cain was very angry, and his face was downcast. . . . Now Cain said to his brother Abel, "Let's go out to the field." While they were in the field, Cain attacked his brother Abel and killed him. (Gen. 4:4–5, 8)

Envy and rejection fueled Cain and Abel's relationship, too. Cain, rejected by God, took his envy out on his brother, whom God loved. The eldest took out his envy on his father when he felt like his father loved his brother more than him. Rejection and envy are two elements always destined to sabotage any relationship, whether it's with a family member or with God.

Carolyn Arends writes,

> I began to wonder if, from Jesus' perspective, having a feast thrown in one's honor is a blessing, but being invited to help the father *host* the banquet is a vastly greater gift. . . .
>
> Maybe the father in Jesus' story felt he could honor and bless his oldest boy more by inviting him into the deep relationship of mutual service than by merely giving him a party of his own.[6]

Jesus loves to party! It's no surprise that Jesus would choose to include a celebration in this parable. In fact, we are invited to a party as well, a great feast when this world comes to an end. Look at Matthew 22:1–14:

> Jesus spoke to them again in parables, saying: "The kingdom of heaven is like a king who prepared a wedding

banquet for his son. He sent his servants to those who had been invited to the banquet to tell them to come, but they refused to come.

"Then he sent some more servants and said, 'Tell those who have been invited that I have prepared my dinner: My oxen and fattened cattle have been butchered, and everything is ready. Come to the wedding banquet.'

"But they paid no attention and went off—one to his field, another to his business. The rest seized his servants, mistreated them and killed them. The king was enraged. He sent his army and destroyed those murderers and burned their city.

"Then he said to his servants, 'The wedding banquet is ready, but those I invited did not deserve to come. So go to the street corners and invite to the banquet anyone you find.' So the servants went out into the streets and gathered all the people they could find, the bad as well as the good, and the wedding hall was filled with guests.

"But when the king came in to see the guests, he noticed a man there who was not wearing wedding clothes. He asked, 'How did you get in here without wedding clothes, friend?' The man was speechless.

"Then the king told the attendants, 'Tie him hand and foot, and throw him outside, into the darkness, where there will be weeping and gnashing of teeth.'

"For many are invited, but few are chosen."

PARTY ATTENDER OR HOST?

As I researched and reflected on this passage, I realized how much meaning is packed into the father's conversation with the son. With great mercy the father pursues the eldest and comes to him, something he doesn't do with the prodigal. Looking at the context in which this passage is written, this is located as one of three parables: the lost coin, the lost sheep, and the lost son. In the parables of the lost sheep and coin, the person goes out in pursuit of what is lost and it is brought back into the fold. But in this parable, that's not the case. By making the prodigal the center of the parable, it seems as if this parable is misplaced, because the father doesn't pursue the prodigal son; he waits and lets the prodigal come to him. But if the eldest becomes the focus of the story, then the parables is right where it belongs, because the father goes out to welcome the eldest back into the fold. Instead of telling him he'll throw him a party too, he says, "Come in and host this party with me." Just like God partners with Adam in the creative process of naming animals and partners with us in preaching, teaching, and being the hands and feet of Jesus, the eldest gets to partner with God in hosting a feast for all his children. Jesus promises that in heaven there will be a great feast to which we are all invited. But Jesus doesn't attend the party; he hosts. He understands the importance of hospitality and its link not only to meeting people's needs but also to salvation.

HOSPITALITY AND THE ELDEST SON

In my last book, *An Invitation to the Table,* I talked specifically about the link between Jesus's ministry on earth and hospitality as a crucial part of that. In fact, hospitality is a necessary part of growth and discipleship. As demonstrated in Luke 9:1–6, the disciples had to rely on the generosity of others to meet their needs, and they were instructed not to take any luxuries with them:

> When Jesus had called the Twelve together, he gave them power and authority to drive out all demons and to cure diseases, and he sent them out to proclaim the

> kingdom of God and to heal the sick. He told them: "Take nothing for the journey—no staff, no bag, no bread, no money, no extra shirt. Whatever house you enter, stay there until you leave that town. If people do not welcome you, leave their town and shake the dust off your feet as a testimony against them." So they set out and went from village to village, proclaiming the good news and healing people everywhere.

The prodigal is much like the disciples in this passage in that he also has nothing. He has to rely on the generosity of his father. I can imagine his fear as he walked home, having lived a wild life and wasted time, money, and everything else. What would his father say? Would he even accept him, welcoming him back with open arms, or would he turn him away and let him do the walk of shame back to the world that had proved worthless?

What does the father do for the son? Throws him a feast! The prodigal son parable is about hospitality, among other things. The dinner table is really the gateway from stranger to brother, and the fact that the eldest is hesitant to eat with the younger tells me that he hesitates to have a strong bond with the prodigal.

We know that his father welcomes him back and the eldest doesn't, but the father invites the eldest into an opportunity to display hospitality and to bond as brothers. In my previous book, I share a story that I'd like to share here:

> "Lord, help me!" the woman from the congregation wailed. Coping with her son's unexpected death proved too difficult to bear. She came up to the altar during the church service, placed her face down into the carpet, and with gut-wrenching cries, wailed, "Lord, help me. I can't take this." Overwhelmed with compassion, I knelt down next

to her and placed my hand on her back, rubbing it gently. No back rub, tissue, or hug could take away this woman's pain, and I didn't try to remove it. I just wanted to be there for her during her time of need.

The woman, sensing my presence, lifted her head and placed it on my chest. I couldn't take away her pain, but I could offer a temporary place for her to rest her weary body and soul. The worship leader, sensitive to the scene, played the same song in a loop until this woman could muster the strength to rise. As I turned to leave, I noticed six other women had come to comfort the woman, all placing their hands on the woman and on each other. Passing around the tissues, we all dabbed our eyes in a single act of solidarity, all bearing this woman's burdens with her, if only for a moment.

What was most interesting about the scene was the woman's desire to seek the help of her church body to comfort her during her time of need. As she cried out to God, she cried out not in a fit of rage but as an act of desperation. As the head of our deaconess board, she organizes all of the annual church suppers, Mother-Daughter teas, and hospital visits. She also regularly visits elderly shut-ins and volunteers at the hospital, singing hymns to the chronically ill and holding hands with those in palliative care. So beloved by the community, the community was now the one holding her hand during her hour of need.

I admire her willingness to come to God with arms outstretched, expecting him to comfort her and give her his peace. I'm not sure I could show that type of maturity in her situation. I would have jumped to the anger

> stage of grief, shaking my fist in the air and begging God to pay me back what I felt he owed me. As I spoke to the woman after the service, she always kept the right perspective, even in the throes of despair. She said, "My son was God's before he gave him to me. I'm thankful for the years I had to enjoy him before God called him home." This woman was allowing her church family to meet her physical needs in order to make way for God to meet her spiritual needs.[7]

This woman in this story knew Jesus. She served faithfully in our church and in our community, and many people spoke highly of her. But it was in the moment when she was at rock bottom, reeling from her tragic loss, that she knew God intimately. She knew him through the people who surrounded her with their outpouring of love, with their prayers, and with their generosity in caring for her son's family through monetary gifts.

I also shared this story in *An Invitation to the Table*:

> In exploring the concept of hospitality, one important element to note in Jesus's receiving of hospitality is his physical posture when he dined with his friends. The Bible cites more than five instances where Jesus *reclined* at their tables. Jewish tradition dictated that he would merely sit at the table. But at special banquets and feasts, like those at a Passover, reclining signified a celebration of life. When people welcomed him into their homes merely to enjoy his presence and not to ask him to meet their needs in any way, he reclined.
>
> To embody hospitality means to relax and welcome a visitor to your table. It may mean to your physical dinner table, or perhaps to a spiritual one in which you open

> your ears to listen to others who need someone to talk to. It may mean sharing a meal with cherished friends, or sitting next to a stranger, someone you would never choose to share a meal with otherwise.
>
> If we embody hospitality, it will become something we *are*, not merely something we *do*.
>
> Hospitality is more than just entertaining friends. It may mean getting to know someone in a deep and intimate way. It means providing an atmosphere in which people can share the deep parts of themselves without fear of judgment or criticism. It may mean telling someone else difficult things about yourself as well.
>
> I believe that, through Jesus, new life comes through our displays of hospitality and our humility to accept hospitality when we need it. Providing for the needs of another person (or being willing to accept help to meet our own needs) is an outward display of the saving work of the Holy Spirit. Furthermore, perhaps it's true that our spiritual growth depends on our humility to supply or receive gifts from a generous God.
>
> Hospitality is not one single gesture but a lifetime of offerings that, when combined, comprise our lives. Hospitality serves as a sign to a dying world that Jesus is the new life they long for.[8]

The eldest knew the father well enough to carry on the family name and care for the family land. But by extending his invitation to come into the party, the father is inviting the eldest to get to know him in an intimate way, to bond with him as father and as brothers, and to experience the joy of intimate fellowship together as a family.

The disciple John had a glimpse of this intimacy too. From resting his head on Jesus's bosom to being chosen to write the book of Revelation, John built a strong bond with Jesus by following him, eating with him, and learning from him. But when John became a pastor, he experienced a bit of pain, too. The three letters of John were written in the midst of a church split. What pain John must have felt when people who didn't like what he was preaching left and took a bunch of other people with them. Having an intimate relationship with the Savior and experiencing the pain of watching him die probably prepared him for the pain of the church spilt he would experience later. John could have pouted, gone out in the field with arms crossed, and tried to control the situation. But instead he writes,

> We proclaim to you what we have seen and heard, so that you also may have fellowship with us. And our fellowship is with the Father and with his Son, Jesus Christ. We write this to make our joy complete. (1 John 1:3–4)

He, like the father, extends a hand to the departed church members in an effort to heal and reconcile the body of Christ. John understood the importance of intimacy and, having had a great example in Christ, he knew that unity with other brothers and sisters was important. The eldest, however, wasn't so sure. He, in the throes of grief, had one thing holding him back from true intimacy—a rebellious heart.

THE ELDEST'S ISSUES: A TIME TO GRIEVE

Think for a moment about the deep losses in your life. Think of a time when you felt extremely rejected, disappointed, or disillusioned with your life. Were you planning on marrying the love of your life, only to hear them say, "This isn't working out"? Did you apply to that college or job only to find that someone less qualified than you got the position? How did those losses make you feel? Angry? Sorrowful? One of the most shocking and sorrowful times in my life was when my mother passed away unexpectedly of a heart attack. I was sitting in my pajamas one chilly night in October thirteen years ago when I received a shocking phone call: *Your mom's not breathing. You need to come down to the hospital.*

When I made my way to the front desk at the hospital, they quickly ushered me to the bereavement room. There I found my sister and father in disbelief. We sat in stunned silence as we waited to hear from the doctors. Fifty minutes later, we received the news no one wants to hear: *We're sorry, but she didn't make it.*

My world was falling apart. No time to grieve. No time to mourn. No time to say goodbye. Having just moved from Canada back to the United States, my husband and I were still unpacking, getting used to our new jobs, and trying to settle into a new chapter in our lives, and this was one page we didn't want to have to read. The world spun around me, and all I wanted to do was make it stop. The grief I experienced but never fully expressed was instead stuffed down deep in my soul, not to be revisited until many years later. Instead, I dealt with daily bouts of emotion, anger, and denial common to someone working through the stages of grief. A few years later, in a moment of intimacy with God, all those pent-up feelings and emotions came bubbling to the surface in a fit of rage.

God, why did you do this?

This is so painful.

I didn't get the chance to say goodbye.

I realized I had not fully grieved the loss of my mother and that I needed to do so in order to be free. Grief is a part of life, and we need to gain closure and properly say goodbye to the things in life we thought we could keep. But the church doesn't do grief well, does it? When I first announced that my mother had passed, so many people tried to offer me words of consolation, but they really only added to my sorrow. One person, a Christian, asked upon hearing the news, "Was your mom saved before she died?" Instead of words of comfort, they offered me some salt to pour over my already raw and wounded heart.

Was the eldest grieving his losses, too? Is that the reason behind his sudden outburst at the end of the story? Consider for a moment all of the losses the eldest had just experienced. He lost his brother, who rejected him by running off to find value and worth in a bunch of strangers rather than him. He received his inheritance, but lost his reputation in the process. He lost the respect of the community when his brother ran off, and his father footed the bill. Perhaps the anger he was experiencing was hurt and grief disguised as rage. It is obvious he is feeling some sort of anger toward his father when he says, "You don't even offer me a young goat . . ." Maybe if he had talked with the father and expressed himself, he could have resolved his jealousy and responded with love instead of resentment. In another chapter, we will explore the eldest's anger toward his father, but for now let's think about the grief the eldest was harboring that may have manifested in a destructive way in his relationships.

Think for a moment about the losses in your life. Have you properly grieved all of them? What feelings or emotions might still remain from your unprocessed grief?

Brent Curtis, coauthor of *The Sacred Romance*, writes,

> Instead of dealing with the arrows, we silence the longing. That seems to be our only hope. And so we lose heart. . . . How many losses can a heart take? If we deny the wounds or try to minimize them, we deny a part of

> our heart and end up living with a shallow optimism that frequently becomes a demand that the world be better than it is. On the other hand, if we embrace the arrows as the final word on life, we despair, which is another way to lose heart. To lose hope has the same effect on our hearts as it would be to stop breathing. If only there were someone to help us reconcile our deepest longings with our greatest fears.[9]

Ron Walborn, Dean of Alliance Theological Seminary, provides some counsel from Henri Nouwen regarding the benefits of processing grief in a positive way:

> Yes, we must mourn our losses. We cannot talk or act them away, but we can shed tears over them and allow ourselves to grieve deeply. To grieve is to allow our losses to tear apart feelings of security and safety and lead us to the painful truth of our brokenness. . . . But in the midst of all this pain, there is a strange, yet very surprising voice of the one who says: "Blessed are those who mourn; they shall be comforted." That's the unexpected news: there is a blessing hidden in our grief. Not those who comfort are blessed, but those who mourn! Somehow, in the midst of our tears, a gift is hidden. Somehow, in the midst of our mourning, the first steps of the dance take place. Somehow, the cries that well up from our losses belong to our songs of gratitude.[10]

REBELLION AND THE ELDEST

It is easy to cite the prodigal's rebellion as the reason why he chooses to leave his father—and why he needed to repent from it. But the eldest was as rebellious as the prodigal—he just didn't show it in the same way. The prodigal was attracted to a new life where drinking long into the night with friends surrounding him, pressuring him to drink a bit more, was his new norm, with loose women hoping to spend more of his daddy's money, waking up to a mid-morning drinking binge, until one day all the money runs out. Then one morning, the prodigal wakes up to no friends, no booze, and a gaping hole in his heart that can only be filled by his father.

Perhaps the eldest felt betrayed by the prodigal. His sudden departure, his desire for a new life, and disdain for his own family in the words, "I want my inheritance now," which amounts to saying, "I wish you were dead." The rebellion grew for the eldest. He may not say he is rebellious, but his heart was filled with anger that came out as words to himself like, "That bum! I can't believe he left me with all this." These words were perhaps whispered in the wee hours of slaving out in the field, trying hard to scrape together a semblance of respect in his community.

The religious spirit grew within his heart as well. The eldest thought he knew what love truly is and what it means to bond as a family, but his heart was so stuffed full of resentment that bitterness had taken root, allowing a poison to permeate every corner. It's amazing to me that the eldest didn't leave to go find his brother, hoping to talk him out of his mistake. As Martha tells Jesus, "Tell her to help me." It would make sense if the eldest said to his father, "Go out and find him. Don't let him embarrass you in this community. You have a reputation to maintain." The religious person has a form of godliness in outward ceremony and ritual, but these things offer no power for a changed life. The eldest did all the right things, as if he was a dutiful son, but his heart was as far from the father as the prodigal's was.

THE ELDEST AND A RELIGIOUS SPIRIT

What is a religious spirit and what does it look like in a Christian's life? Robert Heidler, author of the chapter "The Counterfeit Kingdom" in C. Peter Wagner's *Freedom from the Religious Spirit*,[11] writes about the symptoms that manifest when a religious spirit is present. After each of Heidler's points, I share how the religious spirit can creep into our hearts without even realizing it.

1. There Is an Overemphasis on Outward Form

Keeping up outward appearances is critical if you have a religious spirit. In this way, you can dress in the right clothes, wear the right hairstyle, and use the same Christian language to appear righteous. Yet a spirit focused on behavior rather than the heart always leads to spiritual destruction.

2. There Is a Sense of Condemnation and Fear

The religious spirit always condemns you if you don't "get it right." A continual fear of failure and of being wrong can cause constant worry about whether or not you are a "good enough" Christian.

3. There Is an Alternating Attitude of Pride and Shame

If you are able to keep up outward appearances, a religious spirit will give you a self-righteous pride in your accomplishment. If not, there is often shame attached. But there are two kinds of shame: healthy shame, where you've done something wrong and you feel bad about it, and unhealthy shame, where you've done something wrong and there is something wrong with you because of it. The prodigal dealt with healthy shame—not shame heaped on him by his father, but from his own conscience. The eldest, however, dealt with unhealthy shame, also not placed on him by the father, but from society and its expectations of what a family should and should not do.

4. An Obsessive Focus on the Negative Things That Are Happening around You

In the third year of our church plant, the ups and downs that come with church planting were taking their toll. Our financial future looked bleak, our marriage was on the brink, and my spiritual life was at its lowest point. As someone who at the age of eighteen had to find a new home because my parents threw me out of the house for converting from Catholicism to born-again Christianity, I understood the true cost and loss of becoming a disciple. But watching people go in and out of our church like a revolving door was probably the darkest time in my spirituality to date. I couldn't find anything positive in any aspect of my life. Before I knew it, that religious spirit crept in and took root.

5. A Person That Is Always Trying to Fix What's Wrong with Other People as if They Were Appointed by God with This Mission

Is it just me or are people sometimes one way when you meet them face-to-face and a completely different way on Facebook? I realize social media creates a false sense of reality by allowing us to be such great people in the world's eyes, allowing us to choose what we want people to see. But it has also created an environment where people can say what they want when they want with no filter, therefore ruining their reputation as Christians. I have to confess I struggle with this, too. At times, I am humbled, living in the reality of my wretchedness. When I'm not connected to Christ, however, that can quickly change to a disdain for everyone else's sin. At times, my passion for the church clouds my judgment and I say and do the wrong things in an effort to help someone. But the reality is I can only point to the Holy Spirit, and it's the Spirit's job to convict.

When I feel it's my job to fix someone, rather than point her to the Spirit for conviction, the religious spirit rears its ugly head.

6. A Sense That We Are Closer to God Than Other People or That Our Lives and Ministries Are More Pleasing to God

This is also a tough one for me to overcome. As a pastor's wife for almost twenty years, it is easy for me to think that I am "closer to God" than others because of all the sacrifices I have had to make for the churches we have helped to lead. It's almost like that's my justice for having to sacrifice more than others. Much like the eldest, I have felt that because I did everything God has asked of me, I somehow deserve more favor, more material possessions, etc., as a reward for my hard work. Like the workers that complained to the landowner about the unfairness of giving the ones who worked less time the same reward as the ones who worked the longest, I have also struggled with watching other people who didn't follow the rules or didn't conform to the norms receive the same reward as me. Every time I allow that jealousy to reign, I make less room for the Spirit to work.

7. The Tendency to Compare Ourselves to Others We Think Are Less Spiritual, Thus Building Up Ourselves While Tearing Down Others

During my sophomore year of high school, I ran for student council. I wasn't very popular, but most people knew who I was. My emotional speech persuaded people to vote for me, and I won. As I walked down the hall toward the student lounge to celebrate my victory, I spotted another girl, who had also tried out for student council, sobbing at her locker. I felt terrible that she had to lose so I could win. Later that day, a friend told me that girl was talking bad about me all over school in an attempt to ruin my reputation. She tore me down so she could build herself up.

However, she's not the only one. I know I have torn other people down in terms of beliefs or their treatment of me in an effort to make myself feel better and to puff up my temporarily deflated ego at the expense of someone else's dignity and worth. In my effort to puff myself up, I have instead made myself small, stepping on others to climb the ladder of success and position in order to make myself big, leaving my friends reeling from the pain of my missteps.

The religious spirit is the antithesis of the Christian life. The religious spirit hinders the Holy Spirit from doing its job. It keeps us in a state of pride and arrogance rather than allowing humility and grace to rule our lives. Jesus was right when he said, "For out of the overflow of the heart, the mouth speaks," because the religious spirit that has tainted the heart also taints the words that come out of the mouth (Luke 6:45 BSB).

8. The Tendency to be Suspicious of or to Oppose New Movements, Churches, or Ministries

When I was younger, I grew up Catholic, and then converted to born-again Christianity when I was eighteen. After my conversion, I attended both an evangelical free church and a nondenominational church before joining our current denomination, the Christian and Missionary Alliance. In college, as part of an assignment, I was asked to take part in a cultural exchange in which I attended the religious services, ate the food, and observed the rituals of a culture different from mine. I wanted to attend different church services, so I attended a Jewish service, an African American service, and spent a day with a Vietnamese exchange student. It was one of the most eye-opening experiences I have ever had. I tasted different foods (some I liked and some I didn't) and learned more about why different religions celebrate their beliefs in a different way than I. While it taught me to not focus on just my way of worship but to embrace different means of worship, at the time, I poked fun at the rituals, thankful for the church I attended and how I participated in worship with them. As I reflect on the experience now, I see how narrow-minded I was (and can still be). I only thought of worship in one way, in line with my past experience, which included a short service, little fellowship, and little connection outside of Sunday. What those three experiences taught me was that there are different ways to celebrate and exhibit your beliefs. The African American church was more charismatic than I was used to. I felt awkward as people danced in the aisles, pushed people down who claimed to be "slain in the spirit," and made tithing an entire part of the service. The Jewish service was very reserved, with strict adherence to the Law and the expectation that Saturday was the day dedicated to the Sabbath, and therefore the whole day should be dedicated to the Lord. My experience with the Vietnamese exchange student opened my eyes to different tastes and an emphasis on different values, such as strict closeness with family, respect for elders, and symbolism emphasizing luck and good fortune rather than closeness with God.

My point is this: there are different ways of worship. Everyone is in a different place in their spirituality. It is not fair to expect that someone should worship in the exact same style and tradition as I do. But we can still be in fellowship with each other and at the same time be in communion with him. But when the religious spirit reigns supreme, it clouds my judgment. Soon I don't see people as other brothers and sisters in Christ, but as a problem to fix and a project to take on, as if they're a charity. This is not the way Christ wants us to behave toward each other.

9. There Is an Oppressive Legalism

The religious spirit offers a legalistic system with no flexibility. It wants to produce a method that can replace the dynamics of a relationship. And it causes you to feel like you never measure up. Legalism takes biblical principles one step further. For example, a biblical principle would be that prayer is a discipline which can help you draw closer to God. Legalism, on the other hand, says if you don't show up for a prayer meeting, you must not be a committed Christian.

10. There Is a Need to Figure God Out

Religion without relationship reduces God to a subject for intellectual study. The goal is to understand God and make him predictable. In that process, we miss out on a deep spiritual relationship.

11. There Is a Dependence on Self-Effort

Self-effort allows you to feel as if you're in control. It often leads to comparisons. In another chapter, we will explore the role comparison plays in the eldest's relationship with his brother. But in this chapter, we will simply say that this contributes to a spirit that says what you are or what you have is simply not enough.

12. There Is an Undue Emphasis on Tradition

Ron Walborn says, "Past altars become present idols." While it's great to remember what God has done in the past, we need to be careful that it does not hinder our willingness to change or get in the way of what God is doing in the present. When tradition slips into traditionalism, it quenches the Holy Spirit.

These characteristics can be found in the Pharisees, in the eldest brother, and if we are not intentional about finding freedom from them, in us as well. Our default, apart from the help of the Holy Spirit, is religion.

THE MANIFESTATIONS OF THE RELIGIOUS SPIRIT

C. Peter Wagner, editor of the book *Freedom from the Religious Spirit,* does a fantastic job of explaining the religious spirit and preventing it from wreaking havoc in your life. Wagner speaks about what he calls the modus operandi of the religious spirit and fits it under the following categories: counterfeits the expression of God, denies God's Word and character, upholds tradition over truth, validates hypocrisy, appeals to your flesh, and leaves no room for grace. Following are examples of how I have seen the religious spirit wreak havoc in my life and in the lives of the churches I have led:

Counterfeits the Expression of God

In one of our churches, we were asked to do marriage counseling for a couple wanting to get married. As we met with them, there were no red flags. They said everything we wanted to hear, throwing in the name of God or Jesus every now and then. But something within me said this wasn't right. Despite my reservations, they went through with the wedding and seemed happy. But as soon as their role in church came into question, everything unraveled; within a short time, they were divorced. It is easy to deceive ourselves into thinking we have a deep relationship with God. We can say and even do all the right things, yet be empty on the inside. Satan loves to deceive us by robbing us of the intimacy we deeply desire.

The eldest did all the right things, too. He served and sacrificed, working his fingers to the bone in the name of family loyalty. Yet when it came time to celebrate his brother's accomplishments, his envy took over. In every way, he looked like the dutiful, righteous brother, but the father soon realized he wasn't righteous at all.

Denies God's Word and Character

"Deny" is a harsh word here. It appears a bit more subtle. Maybe it means to doubt what the Word of God says is true. Maybe it's denying that you have interpreted Scripture correctly, or that the person in your church whom you thought was wise is telling you something you don't want to hear. For example, I'm a person who tells it like it is when I speak with people. My passion and care for others sometimes explodes into me being direct with them and helping others be better rather than simply telling them what they want to hear. It is not an easy role to play—and definitely not the most popular. This happened when I tried to help someone realize the source of their lack of connection with God. When I told them what I believed God had revealed, they quickly dismissed it, because it was a difficult admission to make to someone. A few months later, I received a phone call from that person saying that during a time of prayer, the Lord revealed the exact same thing I had told them months before.

The eldest denied God's character, too. It was hard to believe that God would accept and extend grace to someone who didn't look like he did—so he dismissed it instead of embracing it. Although we will never know if the eldest changed his ways, it's easy to see that he needed to take a lesson from his father—to deny his son was to deny God.

Upholds Tradition over Truth

This is something I often see play out in churches. It is always hard when a ministry declines, especially one that has been a part of that church's culture for many years. When attendance goes down and people stop showing up for events or asking about the ministry's status, it is tough for the leader to have to shut a ministry down. However, people who have a passion for the ministry get offended and fight hard to keep it going. But as Ecclesiastes states, "To everything there is a time, a season for every activity under heaven." When a ministry is going under, it is important to let it die for the sake of the health of the church culture. But those who have put their time, energy, and resources into keeping that ministry going feel confused as to what their place is in the church. In their grief, they fight to find their role, and if they find there is no role, they leave the church or try to sabotage the ministries of others. Tradition becomes god instead of them trusting that the death of the ministry is what is best for the church as a whole.

Validates Hypocrisy

Tommi Femrite says it best when she recounts a story in which a Christian realizes her hypocrisy:

> One day we were having a mother-daughter argument, when she yelled, "I hate you! I hate what you are! I hate what you stand for! You're a hypocrite." Her words went like arrows into my heart. I knew that she was right—I was a hypocrite. You see, I could stand before a group of women or a congregation and look so spiritual, sound so wise and act the part. However, I wasn't the same person in my home as I was outside the house. I fact, I thought I could relax and let my flesh hang out when I was at home.
>
> God showed me through the words of my daughter that I was using my home as a place to validate my sin. My home was a place where I could be angry, judgmental, critical and rude. . . . Looking back now, I realize that I was being victimized by the spirit of religion. This

> religious spirit deceives you into thinking that the outward details of your behavior are what counts, not what is deep in your heart. It makes you a hypocrite.[12]

Reading these words are like arrows for my heart, too. I am everything this paragraph says I am. But there is hope. I don't have to be a slave to the religious spirit any more than you do. If you find an eerie similarity between your attitude and that of this Christian mom, you can break free from it, too.

Appeals to Your Flesh

Just as Satan tempted Jesus by appealing to his human desire to be known by others, to appeal to his needs and rely on himself rather than God the Father, it is the same with us. Satan is always appealing to one of those three basic needs. Our sin seeks to fuel our own pride rather than deflate our otherwise inflated egos. The trick is to be equipped with the Word of God, wise counsel, and a dependence on God to resist those temptations. Think for a moment about the relationships with people when you have had an argument, or worse, had to end your relationship with them. Was pride the source of your squabble, or did you seek to elevate someone else above yourself? More than likely, you elevated yourself rather than someone else. Satan knows the exact areas in which you are weak, and he turns up the heat by offering you a way to meet those basic needs without God. When he succeeds, we find ourselves in a worse place than we would have been if we had resisted.

Leaves No Room for Grace

Think about the people you have been in fellowship with at your church. Can you think of someone who is constantly grumbling about the way things are, as if they are less spiritual than they were years ago? Do they grouse about the worship, complain about the pastor's dress, or look the other way when asked to join an up-and-coming ministry? More than likely, they are wrestling with the spirit of religion as well. Pride creeps in, making it easier to talk about someone than talk to them. Complaining and arguing become the new native language, and that person is fluent. As that person influences others, it makes it easy for those around them to hold that same attitude rather than embracing change.

Having no room for grace is the opposite of what God wants to accomplish. Our goal is to abound in grace, not stuff it into a back room where no one can access it. Instead, it should be on display for all to see. A new church attendee should say, "This is a place that welcomed me when I was not living a godly life" rather than, "I stopped going to church because I had a bad experience with someone who told me I was going to go to hell because of my past."

WARNING SIGNS THAT YOU MAY HAVE A RELIGIOUS SPIRIT

Rick Joyner writes about behaviors that act as symptoms of a religious spirit in his chapter "Combating the Spirit of Religion" in the book *Freedom from the Religious Spirit.*[13] If you see these things in your life, there's a good chance the religious spirit is trying to creep in.

1. People with the religious spirit will often see their primary mission as the tearing down of whatever they believe is wrong.
2. They will be inclined to see more of what is wrong with other people, other churches, and so on than what is right with them.
3. They will be subject to an overwhelming feeling of guilt that they can never measure up to the Lord's standards.

4. They will do things in order to be noticed by people. This is a symptom of the idolatry of fearing people more than we fear God, which results in a religion that serves people instead of God.
5. They will tend to reject spiritual manifestations that they do not understand.
6. They will take pride in their spiritual maturity and discipline, especially as compared with others, such as in Luke 18:11–12 where the Pharisee prays, "'God, I thank you that I am not like other people—robbers, evildoers, adulterers—or even like this tax collector. I fast twice a week and give a tenth of all I get.'"

God wants to free us from these things. He wants you to experience revival—that's his heart. That's why Jesus told this parable in the first place. He's actually being very gentle with these Pharisees. If you see this stuff in your life, there is great hope. The apostle Paul was a really good Pharisee. In Philippians 3:5–6 he describes himself as "circumcised on the eighth day, of the people of Israel, of the tribe of Benjamin, a Hebrew of Hebrews; in regard to the law, a Pharisee; as for zeal, persecuting the church; as for righteousness based on the law, faultless." His life was radically transformed when he met the Lord Jesus Christ on the road to Damascus when he began a relationship with Jesus.

FINAL THOUGHTS ON THE ELDEST

The one question we haven't asked about this story is: Why doesn't either brother have a name? The eldest has no name because we could insert any one of our names and still be relevant. Haven't we all been far from the father, hoping everyone around us gets what we think they truly deserve? Haven't we hugged our neighbor in church, put on our Sunday best, and fixed our makeup and hair, pretending everything is okay? When just an hour before, we fought with our spouse, struggled to get the kids in clean outfits, and swallowed our breakfast on the way out the door, only to put a smile on our face when we enter the church? Isn't this what the eldest did, too? He had no church to walk into, but he put on a brave face, did what he was told, and fulfilled his obligation, even when he was gripped by loneliness from the loss of his sibling and the desperate desire for his father's approval.

I'm writing this book because there is hope. Perhaps you saw yourself in those characteristics I listed above. Maybe you think you are doing fine, but soon the Holy Spirit convicts you and you realize you are not doing as well as you think. Whether you have been a Christian forever or you're a new Christian, we are all susceptible to becoming Pharisees. But just as the father invites the eldest to a new way of life, he invites us to a new way of life, too. Perhaps you will find your freedom between the pages of this book. One thing is for sure: there's a party going on, and you're invited.

The question is: Will you attend?

DISCUSSION QUESTIONS

1 Which brother do you relate to in this parable, the eldest or the prodigal? Why?

2 If you said you relate most to the eldest brother, in what ways do you relate to him? Do you know someone who displays the same traits as the eldest brother?

3 How many characteristics of the religious spirit have you displayed over your years of being a Christian? How many have you been able to overcome, and how many do you still struggle with?

NOTES

[1]Carolyn Arends, "The Other Prodigal Son," *Christianity Today,* February 13, 2012, http://www.christianitytoday.com/ct/2012/february/prodigal-son.html.

[2]"Who were the Sadducees and the Pharisees?" Got Questions website, https://www.gotquestions.org/Sadducees-Pharisees.html.

[3]Reggie McNeal, *This Present Future: Six Tough Questions for the Church* (San Francisco: Jossey-Bass, 2003), 28.

[4]Theodore J. Wardlaw, "In Defense of the Older Brother," *Journal for Preachers* 25, no. 2 (2002): 26, ATLASerials, Religion Collection, EBSCOhost.

[5]Casey Groff, "Jesus Wants You to Party," *Intervarsity* blog, October 31, 2012, http://launch.intervarsity.org/blog/jesus-wants-you-party.html.

[6]Arends, "The Other Prodigal Son," *Christianity Today.*

[7]Michelle S. Lazurek, *An Invitation to the Table* (Abilene: Leafwood Publishers, 2016), 59–60.

[8]Ibid. 41–42.

[9]Brent Curtis and John Eldredge, *The Sacred Romance* (Nashville: Thomas Nelson, 1997), 33.

[10]Henri Nouwen, *With Burning Hearts: A Meditation on the Eucharistic Life* (n.p., n.d.), 27–28, as quoted in Ron Walborn, "Part One—Foundations of Spiritual Formation," compiled 2007, http://www.missionsresources.com/Samples/Spiritual_Foundations_preview.pdf.

[11]Robert Heidler, "The Counterfeit Kingdom," in *Freedom from the Religious Spirit,* ed. C. Peter Wagner (Ventura, CA: Regal Books, 2005), 52–67.

[12] Tommi Femrite, "Protecting Your Soul from the Spirit of Religion," in *Freedom from the Religious Spirit,* 93.

[13]Rick Joyner, "Combating the Spirit of Religion," in *Freedom from the Religious Spirit,* 35–51.

Chapter Three

Dividing Up the Inheritance

Jesus continued: "There was a man who had two sons. The younger one said to his father, 'Father, give me my share of the estate.' So he divided his property between them." (Luke 15:11–12)

I've read this story many times, relating more to the older brother muttering to himself while he worked out in the field for little more than mere pennies. But there's a deeper meaning behind this parable, and it is contained in the sentence, "He divided his property between them." I must admit, I never grasped the full meaning of that sentence until just recently. They may seem like ordinary words to you, but they hold great insight into both the older and younger brother's personalities. The father worked to provide for their family so that the children did not have to be bound to anyone through debt. A father's provision was his children's ticket to self-reliance, so they did not get tripped up in debt, forcing them to sell off the land and property the father had worked so hard to attain.

The younger brother cares little about all the hard years the father worked to provide for the family. By asking for his inheritance, it was in essence like spitting on his father, saying, "Forget you. I wish you were dead." The father, in response, had every right to jump up and down, screaming, "*You ingrate! I'm cutting you off from this family.*" Instead, the father gives the younger brother his inheritance, knowing full well he is not going to spend it wisely, thus bringing dishonor to the family name. But God, in his great mercy, gives it anyway.

In this case, however, the younger brother is not the only one who receives his inheritance. The older brother receives his, too. Not only does the father give it, but the older brother accepts! I have no idea how much the inheritance was in monetary terms. All I know is that it was enough for the younger brother to squander. But since the older brother is as rich as the younger brother, a bigger question remains:

Why did the older brother stay?

He was no longer obligated to help the father in the field. Yet he stays. He stays not because he thinks he owes something to the father, but because he owes something to himself.

Darrell Bock, author of *Luke: The NIV Application Commentary*, states,

> The text also warns us through the older brother that activity for God by itself or proximity to him is not the same as knowing him through a relationship grounded in a conscious, humble turning to him. The older brother sees God more as a taskmaster who uses his services rather than as a gracious father. When we come to God on the basis of his grace, humbly recognizing our need for him rather than trying to earn his favor, we

> find the arms of God ready to welcome us in celebration. We risk missing the joy of relationship with God when we turn him into a scorekeeper.[1]

The older brother got so caught up in who owed what to whom that he missed the point of God's great love and forgiveness. Every round of watering and seeding the field was a tick off the scorecard of life. Just as Jacob labored fourteen years to attain the love of his life, so the older brother thought he had to work for every dollar of his inheritance in order to "even the score" between him and dear old dad. What he failed to realize was that an inheritance, like salvation, is a gift from a loving father, who had already labored and paid the price for what he had earned. He wants to give it as a love offering to the two children he loved in life as well as in death, and the older brother was missing the point of both.

The older brother was so caught up in works-based faith, he was missing out on the grace-based love that God was offering both brothers.

Ephesians 2:8–9 sums up this idea: "For it is by grace you have been saved . . . not by works, so that no one can boast." The problem with works-based faith is that it stifles the spiritual growth of the individual. The older brother got so caught up in checking off days and to-do lists that he forgot to enjoy the wedding feast of gratefulness. He had not only become a slave to tending the fields, he had also become a slave to his own bondage of linear thinking.

Larry Crabb puts it best:

> Let me put it more generally. We all want our lives to work well, to become better than they are or to remain as good as they are. When that desire becomes our goal, the objective we most value, then we like to believe the Law of Linearity is operative. We want to believe there is

> an *A* we can do that will lead to the *B* we want. Our lives then become a sustained effort to discover and follow whatever principles will provide a life that lets us feel pretty good. And it sometimes works. . . . But you might end up farther from God. And you *will* end up farther from God if you think of these principles as methods to produce the better life you want.[2]

At a recent conference, after hearing a lesson on the sin of favoritism, I went into quiet time asking the Holy Spirit to reveal to me some of the deeper issues that were keeping me from a deeper life with him. As I wrote in my journal, the Lord brought to mind instances from my past where I felt like I had been "missed" or "forgotten." Within a few minutes, I had filled several pages of my journal. Situations from my childhood and adulthood were contributing to this underlying feeling of being forgotten by God. This was causing an invisible barrier between us. Although I had dealt with all of those situations on an individual basis, they were still contributing to an overall feeling of being unseen and ultimately unloved by God. Once I was done writing, I felt the Lord impress upon my heart that I should rip up each page and throw it into the trash. When I threw out the last page, it was like a weight had been lifted off my soul. I no longer felt unseen or forgotten, but holy and dearly loved.

There are moments when I still struggle with this. Every time I feel cast aside or uncared for, this feeling creeps into my heart and invades my mind. I have to meditate on who God is and read his Word for this feeling to subside. What I believed was a lie from the enemy, and it was keeping me from living the abundant life God had promised me.

This lie was also keeping the elder brother from living an abundant life. He had built himself a cage, locked himself inside, and thrown away the keys. Like me, he felt as if his father didn't love him as much as he loved the other brother, and he was competing for his father's love and approval, grasping at whatever little crumb his father had for him. Instead of basking in all that the father had for him, he wanted what he couldn't have.

Isn't that the way it is today? Instead of reveling in all we *do* have, we choose to focus on the possessions, relationships, and wealth we *don't* have. Instead of thanking God for the little savings we have, we drool over the neighbor's new car he paid for in cash. Instead of being grateful for the twenty years we have been together with our spouse, we longingly gaze at the newlywed couple's apparent love for each other.

The elder brother was no different. Deep down, he wanted to be free to spend *his* money *his* way, in the time and manner *he* chose. Both brothers had wild hearts, not in submission to God or their father, but wanting to break free from the chains they believed were tying them down. God, knowing this, gives them their due in the hopes that maybe they will come to their senses and return to a loving relationship with him, unfettered by chains but choosing to submit to his faithful and loving ways.

Are you trying to earn your worth before God instead of allowing the father to run to you while you are still a long way off?

May this book help you break free from the chains holding you captive.

DISCUSSION QUESTIONS

1 Why do you think the eldest brother stayed to work on his father's property? Was it an obligation because he was the oldest or something else?

2 Have you ever been in a situation where someone stole something from you that was rightfully yours? What did you do about it? How do you think your response does or does not differ from a biblical response God would want you to have?

3 Are you bound by anger and resentment over what someone has that you do not have? What do you think you can do to change that?

NOTES

[1]Darrell L. Bock, *Luke: The NIV Application Commentary* (Grand Rapids: Zondervan, 1996), 32.

[2]Larry Crabb, *The Pressure's Off* (Colorado Springs: Waterbrook Press, 2002), 19–20.

Chapter Four

Out in the Field

Meanwhile, the older son was in the field. When he came near the house, he heard music and dancing. So he called one of the servants and asked him what was going on. "Your brother has come," he replied, "and your father has killed the fattened calf because he has him back safe and sound." The older brother became angry and refused to go in. (Luke 15:25–28)

During Jesus's ministry, he chose to surround himself with people. Whether it was outcasts he could disciple, leaders he could train, or crowds he could heal, he surrounded himself with people. It is interesting that the parable of the prodigal son is located in the Gospel of Luke in chapter fifteen, because six chapters earlier in chapter nine, Jesus sends out his disciples into the world. He says:

> When Jesus had called the Twelve together, he gave them power and authority to drive out all demons and to cure diseases, and he sent them out to proclaim the

> kingdom of God and to heal the sick. He told them: "Take nothing for the journey—no staff, no bag, no bread, no money, no extra shirt. Whatever house you enter, stay there until you leave that town. If people do not welcome you, leave their town and shake the dust off your feet as a testimony against them." So they set out and went from village to village, proclaiming the good news and healing people everywhere. (Luke 9:1–6)

Jesus's mode of discipleship involved disciples going out together to spread the gospel. Even the animals in Noah's ark went two by two! Here are two reasons why Jesus wanted his disciples to not walk alone:

Accountability

One of the most successful weight-loss programs is Weight Watchers. Not only do they have an affordable and reasonable food program, but they also ask members to attend meetings on a regular basis. For those who are doing well on the diets, it must be a feeling of great accomplishment for them to announce to the other dieters that they met their weekly goal. However, those not doing so well probably feel like a failure when they don't meet their goal. The point of stepping on the scale in front of others is so they can help celebrate with you when you meet your goals and encourage you when you don't.

The Christian life works on the same principle. Jesus wanted them to travel together so that someone could "have their back" during the times of persecution, and celebrate with them when they were able to successfully meet the community's needs. If the disciples tried to meander through the Christian life alone, it would be easy for them to get off track, get discouraged, and not accomplish the work of furthering the kingdom. It was probably also good to have someone with them in case they became a victim of someone who wanted to cause them harm.

FELLOWSHIP

Ministry can be a lonely way of life. I can personally attest to this, being a pastor's wife. For many years I have had difficulty making friends because of my position in the church. In an article (reproduced below), I shared with pastors' wives about the loneliness that can accompany the ministry.

> Taking my usual seat in church one Sunday, I looked around to observe the people coming in to find their seats before service began. As I looked to my left, I noticed two women, chatting away with huge smiles on their faces, obviously reminiscing about some inside joke that was only funny to a chosen few. I looked to the right, and I saw two older women, embracing in a friendly hug. Although they had just seen each other the other day, their hug indicated they relished the opportunity to see each other again. As I looked down at my hands laced together on top of my lap, I realized that I wasn't a part of any of the conversations taking place that morning, or many mornings for that matter.
>
> As much as I want to have close friendships, being a pastor's wife puts up this invisible barrier between me and the people within my church. It's a wall no one acknowledges but still exists nonetheless. It's a wall that prevents us from experiencing the same intimate friendships that other members get to enjoy. That wall prevents me from venting to another congregation member when issues and

> tensions arrive amongst its leadership. It's also the same wall that prevents me from rejoicing when the church leadership has just voted to move in an exciting new direction. It's a wall that I try hard to chisel away to see inside people's hearts. But no matter how hard I do, I only get a glimpse inside, as the wall still covers up the majority of their hearts as well as mine.
>
> I don't write this to make you, dear reader, feel sorry for me as a pastor's wife. Although we don't get to enjoy the gift of fellowship as someone's friend, we do get to enjoy many aspects of the ministry that no one else enjoys. For example, I get to watch back stage as a member who chooses to publicly dedicate their lives to God immerses themselves in a tub full of warm water to the sound of joyous claps and cheers. It's also special to console a family as they sit beside a loved one's bedside who is just a few breaths away from being swept away into the loving arms of Jesus for eternity.
>
> I write this to help you understand the loneliness that plagues a pastor's wife's life. It's part of our responsibility to be everyone's friend, but in the process we lose the gift of intimacy close relationships give us. The next time you see your pastor's wife, don't just wave hello. Take her out for coffee and get to know her. Your friendship is a gift she is waiting to unwrap and enjoy.[1]

The life of the disciples must have been equally lonely. They gave up every comfort and luxury to follow Christ. Jesus knew the journey would be tough; that is why he assigned them to go two by two into the towns to preach and heal the sick. In Acts 3, we see the power of togetherness when Peter and John heal the man at the temple gate:

> When he saw Peter and John about to enter, he asked them for money. Peter looked straight at him, as did John. Then Peter said, "Look at us!" So the man gave them his attention, expecting to get something from them. Then Peter said, "Silver or gold I do not have, but what I do have I give you. In the name of Jesus Christ of Nazareth, walk." Taking him by the right hand, he helped him up, and instantly the man's feet and ankles became strong. (Acts 3:3–7)

Isn't it interesting that Peter does most of the healing in this passage? He, who was once a coward afraid to associate with Christ, since his encounter with the Holy Spirit is willing to use his gifts to imitate the work he saw Christ do. Do you think Peter would have been as bold if John had not been with him? Peter had a first-hand view of John's boldness as he rested his head on Jesus's bosom and ran first to find that Jesus had left the tomb. He knew Jesus admired this boldness and he was calling Peter to fulfill his calling as a disciple through his boldness. In this passage in Acts, Peter is now the example of boldness. While Peter might have still exhibited that boldness if John had not been with him, there is power in numbers. This is especially true if your partner has demonstrated what a disciple is, both in public and in private.

God created us not because he needs anything from us, but because he delights in our fellowship. He gave us the gift of other brothers and sisters in Christ so that we can enjoy the same gift of fellowship that he has with us. He wants us to walk this journey together, not in isolation. Isolation is when Satan can seize an opportunity to attack, when we are at our most vulnerable. First John 1:6–8 says,

> If we claim to have fellowship with him and yet walk in the darkness, we lie and do not live out the truth. But if we walk in the light, as he is in the light, we have fellowship with one another, and the blood of Jesus, his Son, purifies us from all sin. If we claim to be without sin, we deceive ourselves and the truth is not in us.

Going out in the community with someone alongside them allowed the disciples to talk, keep each other away from sin, and share life with each other.

The concept of doing life with someone goes back to the first account of life: the story of Adam and Eve. When both people are looking out for each other, the relationship can be mutually beneficial. However, in Adam and Eve's case, it didn't benefit them much:

> When the woman saw that the fruit of the tree was good for food and pleasing to the eye, and also desirable for gaining wisdom, she took some and ate it. She also gave some to her husband, who was with her, and he ate it. Then the eyes of both of them were opened, and they realized they were naked; so they sewed fig leaves together and made coverings for themselves. (Gen. 3:6–7)

Why was Adam silent when Satan was tempting Eve? He knew what God had said, because God told him before she was even created. Yet when faced with the decision to rebuke the devil or remain silent, Adam chose silence. If he had boldly corrected the enemy, the enemy would have fled, thwarting Satan's plan and keeping paradise intact. But because Adam put his own needs ahead of his obedience, Satan was successful.

Ecclesiastes 4:8–12 speaks about the richness of fellowship when compared to the riches of wealth:

> There was a man all alone; he had neither son nor brother. There was no end to his toil, yet his eyes were not content with his wealth.
>
> "For whom am I toiling," he asked, "and why am I depriving myself of enjoyment?" This too is meaningless—a miserable business! Two are better than one, because they have a good return for their labor: If either of them falls down, one can help the other up. But pity anyone who falls and has no one to help them up. Also, if two lie down together, they will keep warm. But how can one keep warm alone? Though one may be overpowered, two can defend themselves. A cord of three strands is not quickly broken.

Jesus's plan was that disciples would act like brothers, celebrating the triumphs of ministry and picking each other up when discouragement was close behind.

But the two brothers in the parable of the prodigal son couldn't be further apart. The older brother, working out his debt to his father, was desperately trying to earn his father's love; the younger brother was turning his back on his family to allow his chained soul to run free. What if they had been closer as siblings? It might have ended up better for them both. The younger brother could have used the older brother's hard work ethic and loyalty to preserve the family name. The younger brother could have taught the older brother to loosen up a bit. Maybe the older brother wouldn't have been so caught up in being a slave if he had enjoyed life a little more. If they had both received and embraced the gift of intimacy their hearts were searching for, maybe they wouldn't have gotten lost in the first place. Each could have kept the other from wandering in the first place.

Donald Miller, author of the book *Father Fiction: Chapters for a Fatherless Generation,* shares an interesting revelation he learned about the leadership relationship:

> I learned a great deal about myself while watching a documentary a few years ago about elephants in a wildlife trust in Africa. There were twenty-five elephants, all of them orphans, and they had been brought to the trust twenty years before. They were becoming teenagers—in elephant years. The girls were adequate, getting along with the other elephants, but there were a few boys who were causing a great deal of trouble. The narrator talked about the frustrations these few elephants were feeling because they had gone into an early musth cycle, which showed up as a green pus running down their right hind leg. This phase produced aggressive and violent behavior, the elephant equivalent of sexual frustration. . . .
>
> It is only at the first musth cycle that a young male elephant leaves his mother and enters into the African wild, searching for a mentor, a guide. The green pus running down his hind leg and his smell like fresh-cut grass alerts an older, fully mature male, that this is a young elephant in need of guidance. Upon finding a mentor, the young elephant's musth cycle ends. The older and younger begin to travel together, to find food together, to protect each other—the older one teaching the younger what elephant strength is for and how to use it for the benefit of himself and the tribe.[2]

It is human nature for people to mentor each other. The older brother could have mentored the younger brother before it was too late. He could have also dealt with his jealousy directly with his brother and resolved it before it had gotten out of control. But just as he did to Eve, Satan deceived the older brother into thinking it was no big deal. Before he knew it, the older brother had remained silent, watching as his little brother turned his back on the family and toward destructive living. Little did he know it was destroying his life, too.

Theodore Wardlaw said,

> The lush, green fields in your life that you have planted and harvested—the successes, in other words, over which you have presided diligently—do you think that you accomplished that all by yourself? Or are they not the gifts of God's grace? The children whom you have brought into the world to clothe and feed and nurture and grow and finally to launch out of the nest—are they not tokens of God's favor? The prodigal brothers and sisters whose lives you have touched and helped untangle—are they not symbols of God's abiding presence with you? . . . And even if your sins are not for the most part flamboyant but frankly a little boring, even if you are here this morning because in fact you have never left home, God forgives you, too. In fact, I believe that it's the sign of a greater grace that God does not have to run down the road to meet you, and to hug you and kiss you and summon a feast for you—because you're already here. And indeed, for you, the feast has already been in progress for quite some time.[3]

The eldest took great pride in all that he had cultivated. Beautiful lush fields, meticulously crafted and maintained. Beautiful crops as far as the eyes could see in beautiful rows. The eldest did all he could, worked his fingers to the bone so that his family name could be preserved—for what? For the younger brother to squander it? Was that really fair to the older brother?

While the father had promised that "everything is yours," in essence, it was the gift of God's provision and inheritance simply because he was the firstborn son. Instead of basking in the rich gifts of God's blessings, however, the oldest chose to wear it like a badge of honor—displaying his works for all to see. Like the Pharisees, he wanted everyone to pat him on the back and cheer for joy because of his outward accomplishments. But inwardly he was hoping to receive the ultimate accolade—the father's attention and approval.

In the next chapter, we will explore how his choice to isolate himself contributes to his refusal to accept his father's love, and that refusal is the key to his downfall.

DISCUSSION QUESTIONS

1 I state two of Jesus's reasons for not wanting disciples to walk alone in their faith journeys—accountability and fellowship. What steps can you take to attain fellowship and accountability in your life?

2 It is clear from the parable that the two sons were not close siblings. What role (if any) do you think isolation and separation played in the prodigal's desire to leave his family?

3 The eldest brother tries to earn his father's love by slaving away for him in the field. Yet we know all good gifts come from God and are not earned on our own merits. What role do you think pride played in the eldest brother's perspective on his desire to work hard for his father?

NOTES

[1]Michelle S. Lazurek, "Connections: The Single Life of a Pastor's Wife," June 24, 2015, SDG website, http://www.solideogloriasisterhood.com/connections-
-the-single-life
-of-a-pastors-wife/.

[2]Donald Miller, *Father Fiction: Chapters for a Fatherless Generation* (New York: Howard, 2010), 22–23.

[3]Theodore J. Wardlaw, "In Defense of the Older Brother," *Journal for Preachers* 25, no. 2 (2002): 26, ATLASerials, Religion Collection, EBSCOhost, 27.

Chapter Five

Refusing to Come In

The older brother became angry and refused to go in. So his father went out and pleaded with him. (Luke 15:28)

"Why do you always favor her over me?" I shouted. At eleven years of age, I had borne the weight of favoritism for too long, and now it was collapsing around me. "Get in your room," my mother snapped back. As I rushed to my room, the dam that had held back my tears broke, allowing the flood of emotion to flow. From the time I was small, I felt like I was living in my sister's shadow. No matter how hard I tried to be my own person, I could never peek through to find out who I truly was. While not explicitly stated, the overall sentiment of "your sister is the favorite" guided most of my life, leading me to live a works-based salvation, believing if I could prove my love to my mother, I would somehow earn her love. Little did I know, I was placing myself in a self-made cage and throwing away the key. No matter how good my grades were or how squeaky clean my reputation was, it was never enough. Conversely, no matter how badly my sister messed up in life, it didn't matter; she was loved all the more.

After I chose to follow God at the age of eighteen, I was able to give my jealousy over to him. I accepted that I would never have the love and approval I wanted, but I didn't need it anymore. I was beginning to see that God wanted to fulfill the role of parent that I longed for. Despite my spiritual awakening, my relationship with my sister still remained one-sided. Although we were civil to each other, there were still some underlying issues between us preventing us from having the rich relationship sisters can have. My relationship with her came to a head when God woke me one night and asked me, "Is this what you want from this relationship?" As I recalled specific instances where she was not valuing me as her sister, I realized I had been sweeping a lot of her mistreatment under an imaginary rug in the hopes that one day she would know God and we could enjoy full reconciliation. But as the Lord pricked my heart that evening, he reminded me that even God doesn't want to be in relationship with those who don't want to truly know him.

Many people trade the intimacy of a rich life with Christ for a genie in a bottle, hoping God will become a magic entity that will cater to their every whim. I understood that I was trading in a deep connection with my sister for a pseudo-relationship, one in which we had the appearance of a relationship, but it was superficial at best. I had to cut ties with her because the toxicity was not only affecting my relationship with her, but also with God. I had to come to the realization that I'd rather have a real relationship with someone than a superficial one, and that if it was not going to go beyond superficiality, it wasn't worth having.

In the parable of the prodigal son, the father allows the son to leave for the same reason. The father could have said no when his son asked for his inheritance, but he chose to bless him with his endowment instead. When the prodigal comes to his senses and returns home, the father welcomes him with open arms. It is interesting to note that the father, knowing what the young son would do with the money, gives it anyway, and allows him to squander it. He doesn't follow him around, micromanaging his every move. He lets him go, cutting ties, because the son only wants him for a superficial relationship. It is not until the son comes to him wanting intimacy that the father welcomes him back. Which leads me to ask this question: Was it the same with the father's relationship with the oldest son? Why did he allow him to stay out in the field while he was making preparations? Why didn't he ask the oldest to help him? The father had the same superficial relationship with the oldest that he did with the youngest. The difference is that the prodigal returned because of his own convictions, while the oldest was still faced with that dilemma: Should he come in and move his relationship with his father and brother from one of superficiality to one of intimacy? The fact that the oldest refuses to go in to the party helps us understand that we all face the same problem. The father goes out to him and extends a hand of invitation, but the oldest refuses it. His refusal to come in not only symbolizes the relationship with the brother, but also with the father. This raises the question: Where did the Pharisees of whom Jesus was making that comparison find themselves in that scenario? Would they choose to abandon their head knowledge of the Law to pursue intimacy with the Father?

Because of the sin of favoritism, it took me many years to fully understand the unconditional love God offers all of his children. If I'm honest, I still struggle with this to this day. I'm not sure I fully understand a love that comes with no strings attached. Anyone who has struggled with the sin of favoritism can relate to my struggle as well. My lack of experiencing God's favor has spilled into every area of my life, like a curse that hangs over me. I may never understand the fullness of God's love unless I learn to accept myself for who I am and understand that I am worthy of love regardless of what I do or don't do in this life. For years, I longed for approval from my mother, for her to give me the "Atta girl!" that I longed for, but never received. This kept me looking for that love in man rather than in the love of God. After the death of my mother, I did some soul-searching. I was able to forgive her for the sin of favoritism that had lined my life and was able to let go of the love I never fully received. Or so I thought.

The sin of favoritism reared its ugly head once more when my husband and I planted a church in our hometown. My husband, knowing the love and approval of his family, assumed God would show his favor on our new undertaking simply because of who he was. The ebb and flow of attenders and the revolving door that our church quickly became placed a heavy burden on our marriage and spiritual lives. After all we had done to serve God, this was what we got? Every passing year, our finances dwindled, our attendees left for greener pastures, and we were stuck in the aftermath of a hurricane that took over every area of our lives. Before I knew it, I had slipped into a cycle of envy and bitterness. Like the elder brother in the parable, soon I was running away from God, far away in the field where no one could find me. I had built a wall around my heart where no one (including God) could find me.

Looking back on this experience, I realized God had brought people to us in situations similar to ours. These were people carrying baggage from previous bad church experiences. In these instances, God was calling us to be doctor and nurse to those wounded from the battle of life with imperfect people. But with financial circumstances of low offerings and pay cuts looming, we used up all the salve ourselves and had none to give anyone else. When we finally closed our doors five years later, I breathed a sigh of relief. With the promise of a new church and with it steady employment, it was the answer to the prayers we had silently prayed all those years before. But it wasn't just a church plant that had closed: the closing of those doors began a new chapter in our lives as well.

For my husband, those doors closing signified a failure that he couldn't undo. It was like a mark on his permanent record, but he couldn't keep the doors of the church open, no matter how much he sacrificed or how hard he tried to convince visitors to stay. Looking back on that event, my husband is grateful for what God did. Of course, if he had it his way, we would have kept the doors open and we would have plugged away, gaining enough regular attenders to warrant the coveted "official church" status. But the closing of the doors of that church closed the door on something else: the need to be approved. All he could do was allow God's unconditional approval to wash over him. Laying down his own childhood baggage, he became a new man. He didn't have to bow to anyone's expectations, including the members of the new church we led. He was finally free—free for God to work on his soul and free to be the man God was calling him to be.

For me, however, the closing of our church doors signified the opposite—it forced me to wrestle with the secret belief that God didn't see or notice me the way he did others. Living a childhood filled with rejection forced me to work harder, allowing nothing to stop me from achieving whatever goal I set for myself. Because if I could just work hard enough, I could be *somebody.* I may have never said it aloud, but I believed it, and belief can rule every life if left unchecked. This belief of not being seen was revealed to me years later at a conference I attended. The instructor asked people to share their stories with other members of the surrounding group. As I asked God to reveal lies that were preventing me from experiencing God's love, I recalled all the moments in my life when I had been second best. Every spelling contest where I came in second, every B+ on my report card, and every year I couldn't claim perfect attendance contributed to me throwing away my dreams because of the pervasive belief that God didn't see me. Since I hadn't earned his favor (or at least what I had reconciled in my heart to be unearned favor), that spilled into my relationships with my husband, my friends, and my family. Unlike my husband, who struggled with not being a success in his family or the world's eyes, I struggled with not receiving God's love at all. The harder I worked or tried to achieve something on my own merits, the further I got from achieving it. When I was able to cry out to God and ask him to deliver me from my sin of working to achieve his approval, God delivered me and gave me the peace I needed. No longer did I have to worry about earning my way to love. I had already gotten it in a way that filled every crack in my broken soul. If I had gotten the answer to my prayers, we would have kept those doors open, because despite how tough it was, it was familiar, and familiar for me is always better than approaching the precipice of the unknown. But God had soul work to do, and he did it in the midst of deep pain, failure, and the huge weight of rejection. Little did we know that we would be better people because of an event that would have appeared to break us, but that instead reshaped us into the people we are today.

Favoritism played a role in the older brother's position with his father and younger brother, too. The father loves the sons equally, blessing them both with their inheritance early. But the eldest sees his brother's disrespect of the father as a wrong that the father should right. But instead, he doesn't; he blesses him. Have you ever watched as someone got blessed even though his deeds dictated otherwise? How did you feel when that happened? The eldest goes out to the field with a chip on his shoulder, allowing envy to take root. The eldest thinks the father is favoring the prodigal, and that sudden switch in position is what is fueling the eldest brother's anger.

In the culture of that time, the oldest brother received many perks simply by being the oldest. Using Jacob and Esau as an example, culture dictated that Esau should have automatically received the blessing from their father Isaac. Yet Jacob tricked his father into giving him the blessing, throwing the entire order of their society into chaos. I have often read that story and asked myself, "So what's the big deal? Couldn't Isaac give another blessing?" But society didn't work like that back then.

Not only was Esau to receive a blessing, but it also showed that Isaac favored Esau. To bless the youngest meant the eldest son was not worthy of favor, that he brought shame to the family in some way. In addition, not receiving a blessing from his father heaped shame on Esau as well. It was as if Esau was not worthy to carry on the family name. In the same way, the eldest son was most upset that the younger, prodigal son was receiving a special blessing when the blessing should have gone to the eldest instead.

Shame and the Eldest

Having said this, nothing can compare to the inward shame the prodigal son must have felt when he asked his dad for his inheritance. Was it that he didn't care about his father, or did his lack of self-control and carnal desires rule his heart? The eldest, willing to fulfill his obligation to care for his family's property (and eventually his father in his old age) stays behind, even though he has already received his share of his inheritance. When the prodigal returns, the eldest could have released him from the guilt his sinful behaviors must have given him. But he doesn't. Instead, he chooses to grumble and complain, keeping the prodigal in bondage to his spiritual plight. He makes it his main mission to tear his brother down instead of building him up, keeping him down instead of elevating him.

The eldest wrestles with his own sense of shame, too. But as we discussed in Chapter Two, there are two types of shame: misplaced shame and proper shame. In the case of the prodigal, he is feeling the conviction of his soul. That is appropriate, because it is the catalyst that lets him repent and turn back to the father. The eldest, on the other hand, has misplaced shame. He is more worried about the shame society has placed on him because of the way the prodigal shamed the family name. That's another thing fueling his bitterness and resentment. This is also why he can't forgive the prodigal and release him from his shame. If the eldest was less concerned with the world and more with the father's love for him, he would have been able to let his brother off the hook.

Isn't that what the church does today? With the gift of forgiveness we have all received, we could release those unaware of the unconditional love of God by extending grace and mercy, trumping their sin. But instead, we continue to hold "the wages of sin" over the unbelievers, rendering them deaf to the call of salvation that God whispers in their ear.

I understand this in my relationship with my sister. No matter how much love my sister received throughout her life, it has never been enough. This causes a rift in our relationship, allowing a secret jealousy to replace the love sisters can share. Because I have achieved much in life (graduating from college, getting married, etc.), it has clouded her perception when it comes to me. Since I am the youngest, it's as if I have received a special blessing too, one she should have received. This has put a crack in our foundation, ripping us apart.

Furthermore, the fact that the prodigal son asked for his inheritance first in a way showed that his father favored the youngest before the eldest. What a blow to the ego! This is where I feel a bit for the oldest son. Although he gets a bad reputation for not celebrating the youngest turning away from his life of sin, it must have been devastating for the oldest to see that even though the father was disrespected, he still chose to give his inheritance to him anyway.

Blogger Jacob J. Prahlow reviews Richard Rohrbaugh's comments on the shame factor present within this parable:

> [Rohrbaugh] immediately notes both the blessing of two sons in the ancient world, as well as the irregularity of a son asking his father for his share of the inheritance before the father's death. Such actions place the son in dangerous waters because they indicate that he has little sense of familial shame or loyalty. However, when the father gives into his son and grants him the share of inheritance, the situation worsens. Not only has the son questioned the family's honor, but the father, in granting his son's request, has damaged, if not destroyed, the wider familial honor in the community by exposing all fathers with sons to this dangerous economic possibility.[1]

Joseph must have also felt this way with the heavy weight of rejection he experienced when his brothers sold him into slavery. He, too, had to live up to the favoritism placed upon him by his father.

> Now Israel loved Joseph more than any of his other sons, because he had been born to him in his old age; and he made an ornate robe for him. When his brothers saw that their father loved him more than any of them, they hated him and could not speak a kind word to him. Joseph had a dream, and when he told it to his brothers, they hated him all the more. (Gen. 37:3–5)

When he was thrown into the pit, he lost his desired place as the favorite child and had to allow God to remake him into a man who looked to God for his love and approval. In true godly fashion, he raised Joseph up as a cupbearer and eventually allowed him to rule over the land in the midst of great loss of food and wealth. Who better to handle a situation like this than a man who could no longer go to his father for aid, but could only trust in God to guide and direct him? Who better to care for a land under its weight of loss and failure? It is in the deepest pain that God can mold us into the Christlike character he desires, but only if we will let him.

THE RELIGIOUS SPIRIT AND ISOLATION

Perhaps that was what the oldest brother was feeling, isolating himself out in the field, doing for God instead of being with him. His pain at his father's heaping societal shame on him must have made him feel as though the father cared more about the son than he did society's perception that forced him to keep his distance, not only from his dad, but also from God. His refusal to come in to celebrate with the younger son speaks to the state of the older brother's soul. Not receiving what he thought he deserved must have been a difficult pill to swallow. After all, society dictated that he would enjoy the coveted top spot all his life, simply because of birth order. But instead of spending time with God, crying out to him and bringing to him his greatest losses, he took his farming tools and did what he had always done: worked. He believed what I believed, that if I could just work hard enough, I would earn back my coveted spot. This led to jealousy and envy that blinded him to the celebration waiting for him, if only he would take the time and put down his tools. Perhaps this is what Jesus meant when he said, "Look, the harvest is plentiful but the workers are few." The work of salvation is there in front of us, but it usually requires us to put down our own ways of getting the work done and to open our eyes to the work God wants to do in our lives.

The religious spirit always leads to isolation. Instead of walking in love with brothers and sisters in Christ, unified in the goal of spreading the gospel to the ends of the earth, we isolate ourselves, stepping up and positioning ourselves on a high pedestal where no one can reach us, like a king taking his rightful position on the throne. Then with our scepter, we rule on whether or not a person is worthy to walk with us on our spiritual journey. While judgment is an important part of the church's role not only in society but also in helping our brothers and sisters grow, we can't fulfill our role of growth if we are isolated, trying to live out our salvation on our own. What if the older brother had served as a mentor to his younger brother? What if the younger had received the love from his older brother from the beginning of his life? Would the prodigal have been looking to sow his wild oats with the seeming love and temporary approval of other people? Would he have taken his role as caretaker of the family property more seriously?

Jesus never let disciples do life on their own. They were always sent two by two to further the work of the kingdom. I can imagine it is partly to protect each other from the potential danger that persecution may have caused them. But I'm sure it was also to keep each other on the straight and narrow, not giving in to the devil's schemes, and to keep them on the path toward righteousness. It is interesting that Jesus tells this parable in the midst of potential believers, but also Pharisees, who scoffed at his message. The point of the parable is clear as well as open-ended: Will the hearer choose to release those suffocating under the weight of their sin, or keep them tied to their bondage? The Pharisees held their knowledge of the Bible and seemingly righteous behaviors over the head of society, not allowing them the same grace and mercy Jesus was offering them.

WHERE ARE YOU?

Matthew 6:19–20 says, "Do not store up for yourselves treasures on earth, where moths and vermin destroy, and where thieves break in and steal. But store up for yourselves treasures in heaven, where moths and vermin do not destroy, and where thieves do not break in and steal." Yet, it seems moths have come in and destroyed the oldest's treasures of contentment and gratitude. The people in Malachi also remained silent when flawed offerings were being passed off as acceptable:

> "A son honors his father, and a slave his master. If I am a father, where is the honor due me? If I am a master, where is the respect due me?" says the LORD Almighty.
>
> "It is you priests who show contempt for my name.
>
> "But you ask, 'How have we shown contempt for your name?'
>
> "By offering defiled food on my altar.
>
> "But you ask, 'How have we defiled you?'
>
> "By saying that the LORD's table is contemptible. When you offer blind animals for sacrifice, is that not wrong? When you sacrifice lame or diseased animals, is

> that not wrong? Try offering them to your governor! Would he be pleased with you? Would he accept you?" says the LORD Almighty. (Mal. 1:6–8)

The father's pleas in the parable are an extension of that same invitation God gives to the leaders in Malachi: come clean, repent of the ways you have failed, and come join me so we can celebrate! The father has two sons who are lost, and one is found—the prodigal who came to his senses. We still don't know what the response of the eldest will be.

If this were you, which would you choose to do: Bang the gavel like a judge and declare the prodigal guilty, or declare him not guilty and extend the same grace to his brother that God has extended to you?

DISCUSSION QUESTIONS

1 How do you think the sin of favoritism played a role in the oldest's envy and jealousy of his brother?

2 How do envy and jealousy cloud your judgment of God, others, and the world around you?

3 How would the eldest being part of a community keep him from isolating himself from his family?

NOTE

[1]Jacob J. Prahlow, "Parable of the Prodigal Son: Richard Rohrbaugh," *Pursuing Veritas,* August 14, 2014, accessed March 21, 2017, https://pursuingveritas.com/2014/08/14/parable-of-the-prodigal-son-richard-rohrbaugh/.

Chapter Six

Works-Based Salvation

When my husband and I first began our pastoral ministry, we knew nothing about how to lead a church. There was no training manual or anyone willing to mentor us into the position, so we had to learn by trial and error. One of the ministries that was not doing well was our women's ministry. It consisted of a monthly meeting that emphasized fellowship, teaching, and understanding our missionaries who serve in different parts of the world as a part of our denomination. Although it was a worthwhile ministry, it suffered from low attendance and a lack of volunteers. Reviewing the ministry's sustainability, we just believed it would not sustain itself and remain viable. When we spoke to the leader, she said she had led it for years and wanted to take some time off to allow someone else to assume a leadership position. When no one emerged to lead it, the leader agreed to take a year off and see if by next year the ministry would resurrect itself.

The few loyal attendees were upset at this development. They came to the leadership. "I can't believe you are going to let this die after so many years! After all we have done!" We couldn't believe our ears. Why would anyone allow a ministry to remain even after it was failing? As we understood church culture, we learned that those who had put their hard-earned time and resources into the ministry were grieving over their loss, not only of a once growing ministry but of a time when they were most needed. Now that culture had shifted and those once useful ways of doing ministry no longer worked, these faithful church members were at a loss as to how to reclaim their usefulness.

Reggie McNeal, author of the book *The Present Future: Six Tough Questions for the Church,* spoke at a district conference of the Christian and Missionary Alliance, talking about various generations and how their cultures shape how they react to the Word and church. He began by explaining the culture of the baby boom generation, those he calls "builders" because they were the people who built the churches we have today:

> Builders were the ones who learned how to create the manuals, and if you just used a kit, the magic would happen. And that worked for a while when the world was still homogeneous and you still had a Norman Rockwell world and all that. But let me tell you why the builders are stressed and why they are struggling with the changes you make and they are angry, and they don't even know this. Builders are grieving, and that anger they are experiencing and they are pushing back from the changes you are making is . . . .

> You gotta understand that anger is a part of the grieving cycle. So many churches are just stuck in the anger part of the grief cycle. So every week they beat their chest and they rebel against the world out there because they believe we have lost the culture, and there's a surge that the stuff we had in place, the predictability we've buttoned down and bolted it down, and now the floor is coming up with it.
>
> What you have to do with builders is you puncture their grief and help them articulate what it is they are grieving over (or what they perceive as a loss), and help them shift their grief over lost opportunities and help them create a legacy that lasts, because builders are asking themselves, "Have I made a contribution?" "Have I given my life to something that doesn't matter at all?"[1]

Jan Orndorff wrote,

> Look at it from the older brother's point of view. From his perspective, this story does not seem very fair. He had worked hard all his life. It started back in grade school. While the older brother was slaving away on all his homework every night, killing himself to get "A's," the younger brother was goofing off, being the class clown, never doing any work, and still sneaking by with "C's." While the older brother was doing his best to follow all the rules, the younger brother was in the boy's room smoking, writing graffiti on the walls, and getting into any kind of trouble he could.[2]

This is a part of the older brother's problem, too. In his world, society made strict rules that, when followed, created the happy life he desired. If the older brother just worked the field and put in his time, the land and everything in it would be his. But his younger brother came and messed everything up. He wasn't supposed to get his piece of the pie first. He wasn't supposed to be first to get his inheritance. The prodigal was supposed to wait and watch as his older brother got what was coming to him, and he would cheer him on and be happy for him. But instead, he stuck the oldest with the responsibilities of the land and the home. He didn't offer any help or loyalty; he saddled him with the responsibility of taking care of everything. Much like the baby boomers, the older brother is raising his fists to the sky, shouting, "Why are you letting him get away with this? Don't you care about his carelessness? Where is his justice? He gets a party while I slave every day for the rest of my life!"

Tim Keller, author of *The Prodigal God*, said,

> Elder brothers expect their goodness to pay off, and if it doesn't, there is confusion and rage. If you think goodness and decency is the way to merit a good life from God, you will be eaten up with anger, since life never goes as we wish. You will always feel you are owed more than you are getting. You will always see someone doing better than you in some aspect of life and will ask, "Why this person and not me? After all I've done!" This resentment is your own fault. It is caused not by the prosperity of the other person, but by your own effort to control life through your performance.[3]

I've struggled with earning people's love through my performance as well. One of the most difficult parts of my relationship with God has not been acceptance of myself, but my acceptance of who *God* is. My childhood was filled with people who demonstrated approval or disapproval based on conditions. "If you do this, then I will do this . . ." When I didn't live up to that expectation, love was withheld from me. So I learned to view love through a works mentality. The harder I worked, the more love I received. If I got good grades, said the right things, did chores without complaining, then I would win my parents' approval. When I grew up and began my relationship with the Lord, I had difficulty viewing God as a Father who loved me for me. If I'm honest, I still struggle with this today.

After living so many years in a works-based relationship, it is hard to accept that even when I'm not perfect, God still loves me. Perhaps it is difficult for you to accept yourself for you, too. But you can't love God fully unless you love yourself fully. For so many years, I believed that if I just did the right things—went to church, worked hard, persevered during the hard times—God would magically reward me with whatever I wanted (or at least what I thought I wanted). So many times God has demonstrated to me that I cannot hide behind my strengths to make up for my weaknesses.

When I went for my master's degree, I worked hard completing classes. As I stated before, I did well in school and wore my intelligence like a badge for all to see. But as I trudged through class after class, I couldn't get an A in any of my classes. The teacher's assistant that would grade the papers always found something wrong with what I had written, giving me a B or C. Each semester, my GPA dropped lower and lower, to the point where I was on academic probation because my average was not meeting the minimal requirements to stay in the program. I panicked. I prayed; I bargained; I begged. Surely God would let me graduate after all my hard work, right?

It came down to my final classes. Although my other classes were completed online, I had to take two at the actual campus.

Dragging my two young children and making the long eight-hour trip to campus with my husband, I almost didn't want to finish. I attended my second-to-last class cradling an eighteen-month-old toddler and a seven-week-old baby! Before you question my sanity, please know that my husband was gracious enough to watch the kids while I attended class. I wanted to finish and not procrastinate, because I knew if I didn't, my temporary break might become a permanent one, wasting all that time and hard work. Exhausted physically and emotionally, I got my final grade back for the class, and it was a C. It was over. I could no longer stay in the program, and I was in danger of not graduating. As we drove that eight-hour trip home, tears streaked my cheeks as I watched my dream of obtaining a master's degree slip through my fingers. I took it to God and asked him why I couldn't have that degree. He revealed to me that I had been hiding behind my intelligence. God, who gently corrects his children, was stripping me of my façade and letting me know that I could no longer be viewed as intelligent. Naked and exposed for him to see, I repented of my false ways. I asked God to help me accept the fact that I would not receive my degree after all.

Two weeks later, I received my last grade of the year, my final grade of the entire program. I received my coveted A! I stared at my report card in disbelief. After all that work, it had finally paid off! After I talked with the head of my department, they still let me graduate on time. To say I was appreciative of God's goodness and provision was an understatement. Although my motives were wrong in that I wanted to flaunt my master's degree as I had so many other times when I had succeeded in school, God's love for me outweighed my wrongful indiscretion. If I had not received my master's degree, would that have made me any less intelligent in God's eyes? No! Yet, I chose to view my intelligence based on what I had *earned* rather than on God's *grace.* I failed to see my degree as a gift from God and chose to wear it as an invisible badge for all to see.

God had to strip me of my invisible badge of intelligence to help me understand my true worth in him. Unaware, I had built an idol: that only my intelligence could make me seem worthy in others' eyes. Yet, God wanted to strip me of my works-based salvation and replace it with the grace-filled, meritless salvation Christ offers us all on the cross. If I'm honest, I still struggle with letting go of my merits and finding my worth simply in who God has made me. The difference between the older brother and me is, I still have the opportunity to change. The parable never states whether the eldest goes into the party after the father's declaration that he has found his son. But an invitation still waits for me.

And it waits for you, too.

THE GREAT ROLE REVERSAL

A works-based salvation is seen throughout the Bible. One of the passages where works-based salvation is most apparent is the parable of the workers:

> For the kingdom of heaven is like a landowner who went out early in the morning to hire workers for his vineyard. He agreed to pay them a denarius for the day and sent them into his vineyard. About nine in the morning he went out and saw others standing in the marketplace doing nothing. He told them, "You also go and work in my vineyard, and I will pay you whatever is right." So they went.
>
> He went out again about noon and about three in the afternoon and did the same thing. About five in the

> afternoon he went out and found still others standing around. He asked them, "Why have you been standing here all day long doing nothing?"
>
> "Because no one has hired us," they answered.
>
> He said to them, "You also go and work in my vineyard."
>
> When evening came, the owner of the vineyard said to his foreman, "Call the workers and pay them their wages, beginning with the last ones hired and going on to the first."
>
> The workers who were hired about five in the afternoon came and each received a denarius. So when those came who were hired first, they expected to receive more. But each one of them also received a denarius. When they received it, they began to grumble against the landowner. "These who were hired last worked only one hour," they said, "and you have made them equal to us who have borne the burden of the work and the heat of the day."
>
> But he answered one of them, "I am not being unfair to you, friend. Didn't you agree to work for a denarius? Take your pay and go. I want to give the one who was hired last the same as I gave you. Don't I have the right to do what I want with my own money? Or are you envious because I am generous?"
>
> So the last will be first, and the first will be last. (Matt. 20:1–16)

Can't you completely relate to this parable? If it were me in this passage, I would have been grumbling along with the workers hired at the beginning of the day, shaking my fists and demanding better pay because "it's not fair." In my mind, the ones that worked the hardest should get the most reward. But in God's kingdom, all of us are offered the same gift of salvation, whether it is when we are a small child or on our deathbeds.

The workers couldn't understand why other people who worked a shorter time received the same reward. That's classic Pharisaic thinking. The Pharisees thought that because they were experts in the Law, all the rewards of the kingdom could be theirs. Because of their known status in society as experts, they took it upon themselves to decide everyone else's status, too. As long as someone wasn't doing better than they were, they could continue to lord their expertise over everyone else. Envy has a way of creeping into an already content situation. The minute people compare themselves to someone else's fame, intelligence, or attractiveness in an area and fall short, envy seeks to worm its way in, creating division where there should be unity and superiority where there should be humility. That's what these workers struggled with. "Are you envious because you are so jealous?"

The landowner's last statement, "Don't I have the right to do what I want with my money, or are you envious because I am generous?" is one I would have imagined the father saying to the oldest son. Appalled by the eldest's lack of gratitude for all he has already received, I can imagine the father in his frustration uttering this statement to him, forcing him to comply. The beauty of the prodigal son passage, however, is that the father's gentleness transcends all of the sons' actions from the first part of the story until the last word; an open invitation still awaits the eldest, and it is his choice whether or not he will take it.

During those days I worked at a daycare while we planted a church, I did my job to the best of my abilities, and it showed. When a worker in another classroom quit, the director asked if I wanted to become the new head teacher. I was honored and thought the skill set matched my gifts, so I said yes. However, a couple of coworkers became jealous of my work ethic and sudden promotion. Outside on the playground, I saw a child (not from my class) misbehaving. When I tried to stop him, one of the teachers grabbed his hand and said to me, "Pay attention to your own kids. I don't want my kids around a teacher who disciplines kids the way you do." I was floored! I immediately went to the director, who informed me that this teacher had been spreading rumors about me, saying I was disciplining kids in ways that went against policy. When the director questioned me and investigated, she soon found that there was no evidence whatsoever to suggest mistreatment. Regardless of the findings, I felt undermined and sabotaged. What hurt the most was that this was a friend of my husband and me, and we often got together after work at each other's homes. When I confronted him, he gave excuses as to why he had tried to slander my name and reputation, but it was obvious that he was jealous because he wanted the head teacher position; when he didn't get it, he spread rumors in an effort to get me fired.

When I first learned of the allegations, I graciously spoke to the teacher in private, asking him to please stop doing that, and that I had forgiven him and would not hold it over his head any longer. He agreed, and we continued to work together. When it happened again, I knew I had to be firmer. I called a meeting with the director to air our grievances. Within five minutes, his claims were refuted, and he had no basis for his accusations. He was speaking out of envy and jealousy and an "it's not fair" attitude. Unfortunately, due to his constant sabotage and undermining, we had to part ways in our friendship and he quit the job shortly afterward.

We can live our lives with our arms crossed, kicking at sand and exclaiming "It's not fair!" when someone gets something we wanted, or we can live in the reality that God's plan for us may not be God's plan for someone else. God embodies justice, so there is nothing we can do to enlist God's help in pursuing that justice. No amount of pouting, brooding, or manipulating God into doing what you want will change that. God chooses to whom he will grant grace and mercy and who will receive swift consequences for their actions.

THE RELIGIOUS SPIRIT AND WORKS-BASED SALVATION

I have had a heart to lead women's ministry in each of the churches I have served in during our time in ministry. However, who I ask to help me has been crucial in how successful the ministry is. I have the gift of leadership and organization. These two gifts combined trick me into thinking I can organize and launch a successful women's event on my own. However, I know I need to train up leaders to not only help me in my current endeavors but also to take over the ministry if God ever calls me to something else. But one retreat I tried to plan, I picked the wrong people to help me plan it. Everything I did, my helper undermined and sabotaged my work. No matter how organized I tried to be or how I assumed a leadership role, my team made alternate plans, changed meeting times, and talked to people about me rather than talking to me. It was a mess. Although God was gracious and the retreat went well, my leadership balloon had been deflated by people I thought I trusted. I had a choice to make: I could either hold these members in contempt for what they had done to me or I could forgive them and move on with my ministry. For a while, I did nothing, leaving my invitation to forgiveness open-ended, just like the eldest. But as I reflected on all that God had done for me, I realized that my lording my goodness over others is just as bad as their attempts to sabotage my work.

This is where the religious spirit kicked in, on both of our parts. On my part, I was afraid my reputation would be ruined if people talked about me, because then I would not be taken seriously. On the team's part, they felt threatened by my leadership role and believed the lie that there was no part for them in the kingdom. Fear is a big component in the religious spirit Satan uses as a barrier to what God wants to do to advance the kingdom. C. Peter Wagner says,

> In order to accomplish its purposes, the corporate spirit of religion administers what could be described as an intravenous injection of fear. Old-wineskin leaders fear losing their positions of power. They fear being pulled out of their comfort zones. Their typical question is, "What am I going to lose by moving into God's new times and seasons?" They rarely ask, instead, "What is the kingdom of God going to gain?" They are hesitant to risk the possibility of either losing control or losing money. So they capitulate to the religious spirit and do whatever it takes to preserve the status quo, while honestly thinking that they are doing God's will.[4]

Fear has no place in life, whether it is corporate in terms of the church or as individuals in terms of being used to advance the kingdom. Fear had crept into the oldest brother's mind and heart. He wasn't just angry about the prodigal's misdeeds; he feared that if the father allowed it to happen, the oldest brother's work in keeping the property as well as his position as the blessed one would be jeopardized. He never asked what the family would *gain* by the prodigal's return, but only what he *lost*. In the end, if that feeling was not addressed, it would wreck any chance for reconciliation, peace, and harmony the prodigal and the father were working so hard to create.

I bet the eldest felt a bit like this, too. No matter how much hard work he had done to maintain the family's property, in one moment the prodigal had thrown it all away. I can imagine the eldest crossing his arms in front of his chest, kicking the dust from the meticulously manicured field, muttering, "It's not fair! Why are you letting my brother get away with this? He's sabotaging my hard work." While it's true that Jesus would have advocated for the eldest to forgive his brother and move on, I find it interesting that the prodigal asks for forgiveness from the father, but not from his brother. Was the prodigal that oblivious to the fact that his actions had as great a negative impact on the older brother as they did on the father? As the eldest, we can assume he would be wiser and more mature and would forgive regardless of the prodigal's failure to ask. But we know by the eldest's actions that he doesn't have the maturity he should have. The eldest could rejoice in his brother's turn toward righteousness, but instead he takes "an eye for an eye" approach to life, treating his brother in accordance with his actions, not with the abundance of grace he has received from God.

Perhaps that is the problem in all this. Does the eldest actually recognize his own need for grace from the father? Does he realize he is acting the same way his brother is, squandering what he has received, except instead of possessions and wealth, he is throwing away his grace?

On the website Incourage, I shared my story of how the death of our church plant caused me to throw away my grace once my possessions were lost:

> Going through the mounting pile of bills, I logged into my bank account to balance the checkbook. A negative

sign appeared next to the words "account balance."
Staring at the blinking cursor next to the amount, I mumbled to myself: *Doesn't God care about our finances?*

Jesus said not to worry about tomorrow (Matt. 6:25).

But all I can do is worry. How will I care for the family God has entrusted to me?

That's what I said to myself, but in my mind was where the true colors shined: *God owes me more.*

After all the years I have worked for the Lord, and this is what I get? I deserve better than this.

After twelve years in ministry, we had just closed the doors on what we thought was going to be a growing church plant. Decrease in attenders took a toll on us financially, mentally, and worst of all, spiritually. My mind and heart had given up on ministry, and eventually God.

Where was God when I needed him the most?

It's tough to hope and trust in God when life looks bleak. But in the years when service took more out of me than I had to give, I realized that hope is not a magical charm to hold onto, nor a nightlight that shines to illuminate an otherwise darkened room.

Hope is a day-by-day, and sometimes moment by moment, belief in the unseen.

Hope isn't about white knuckling my way through life, struggling to remain in control of an otherwise out of control situation. Like Moses who stuck his toes in the water before the sea parted, so do we who put our hope in a God whom we've never seen, but know is there. For us it was the desperate prayer of "Help us, God," I tossed up to God every week we opened the doors to our church.

> Hope is the belief that God will provide, protect, and work things out for his good, even when things for me are not so good.
>
> As we pulled out of our driveway having lost our home and having to find another church, it seemed all hope was lost. But what I didn't know was that hope was right around the corner. It came in the form of a pantry full of food in a home that we didn't have to pay for, a great benefit after we lost our home. It came in the cards that filled our mailbox welcoming us to our new church. It also came in the form of new friendships and a church hungry for vision and direction.
>
> I could have taken all that for granted if I had kept my former attitude of God owing me something. But instead I grabbed a hold of hope and held it in my hands, placing my belief in the unseen and unknown.
>
> Hope is just around the corner. You just have to believe it's there.[5]

Even God had room for those who complained that they deserved more pay for working longer in the kingdom. God makes room for leaders who lead with a religious spirit. He even has room for someone like me who forgot to trust God and who thought he had forgotten me. There's room for them, there's room for me, and there's room for you. All God asks of us is to trust in his provision and bask in his love and approval, realizing that he loves you simply because you are you. The eldest needed an attitude adjustment, but still received an invitation from the father, and so do we.

All we have to do is stop working for his approval and accept the gifts he offers us.

DISCUSSION QUESTIONS

1 In what areas of your life have you been slaving and you feel God owes you a celebration?

2 How have you viewed your work ethic, particularly in ministries within the church?

3 Have you viewed your service as something that you base your worth upon, or something you give back as an act of gratitude for all that God has done for you?

4 Do you need to readjust how you view your worth in society so you can experience the freedom the prodigal son experiences?

5 Are there ministries you need to let go of because they are holding you back from true freedom in Christ?

NOTES

[1]Reggie McNeal, "The Present Future," speech delivered at the New England Christian and Missionary Alliance District Conference, Wakefield, MA, March 2005.

[2]Jan Riehl Orndorff, "What about the Older Brother?" *Brethren Life and Thought* 50, no. 1–2 (2005): 43–47, ATLASerials, Religion Collection, EBSCOhost.

[3]Timothy Keller, *The Prodigal God* (New York: Riverhead Books, 2008), 60.

[4]C. Peter Wagner, "The Corporate Spirit of Religion," in *Freedom from the Religious Spirit*, 21.

[5]"Holding Onto Hope That's Just around the Corner," *Incourage* website, July 13, 2016, http://www.incourage.me/2016/07/holding-onto-hope-thats-just-around-corner-michelle-lazurek.html.

Chapter Seven

This Son of Yours

But when this son of yours who has squandered your property with prostitutes comes home, you kill the fattened calf for him! (Luke 15:30)

In the movie *Joy,* Jennifer Lawrence stars as Joy Mangano, a broke single mother who gets an idea to put a new spin on an old idea: she invents the first self-wringing mop. In over her head in debilitating debt, divorce papers, and two children, she sells her idea to the head of QVC, Neil Walker, who tries to sell it on QVC, but without success. Determined to see her product succeed, she asks to sell the product herself on the show. She watches in amazement as customers buy her product, enamored not only of its super absorbent cotton and durable plastic design but by her down-to-earth demeanor. In one scene, while she's watching her product tank in sales on live television, her sister sits next to Joy, gloating, declaring, "It's over; you won't get a second chance."

I couldn't help but think of the prodigal son parable as I watched this film. Every time Joy hit a roadblock in the process of making her invention a reality, her older sister watched with an "I told you so" expression on her face. Never could she be happy for the success her sister was having; instead, she thought only of herself, as she had an idea for an invention she was designing with their father.

It was the same for the oldest brother in the parable. It didn't matter that the prodigal had returned home, allowing forgiveness to set him free from the burden of shame and guilt from his wild ways. It didn't matter that once those pig pods hit his belly, the prodigal knew he had hit rock bottom. It didn't matter whether it was his starvation or a repentant heart that brought him back to his father's arms; all he knew was that the comfort of those arms was better than the mud pile he'd found himself in just a few days before. None of that meant anything to the eldest because he was never going to allow the prodigal to get out of the mud pit, figuratively speaking. In fact, he liked his brother there. Because that was where the eldest could lord his success and righteousness over the prodigal's head. If his father celebrated his younger son's new life, the other towns would get wind of it. This would jerk the eldest off his self-made pedestal and replace him with the prodigal, stealing the eldest's place in the spotlight.

John Dubler writes,

> The general types in this parable: The spiritual state of the prodigal brother rises during the parable while the spiritual state of the older brother falls. The father remains constant. He demonstrates love toward both and is consistent in demonstrating the love of God. He is a type of our heavenly Father. The younger son

> represents prodigals everywhere while the older brother represents all those who, through hardness of heart and meanness of spirit want to bring down judgment on all those who are trying to make straight their paths.[1]

I can relate to the older brother in his attempt to keep down his younger brother. Because my sister was favored, it always caused an invisible divide between us. Jealousy was at the forefront of our relationship for many years. I did not realize that this was affecting my life until I attended a recent spiritual life conference. Dr. Rob Reimer encouraged the audience to analyze our lives and reflect on past events. God recalled to my mind many times when I felt second best to my sister, constantly living in her shadow. Because of those events, I was carrying jealousy and envy, which were hindering my spiritual growth.

In fact, every time I lost something or came in second in something, I put an invisible check on my list of ways in which God had wronged me. For example, I was pretty good in school and received good grades. Because of this, I was chosen to compete in my school's spelling competition. I had to compete against another girl in my class. When the competition began, we went head to head for several rounds, increasing both my chances of going on to the schoolwide competition as well as my ego! When it came to spelling the word "surveillance," I thought I had it all sown up. But when I spelled it with a "c" and an "e" instead of an "s" and a "u," I was shocked. The other girl spelled it correctly. Another time was when I was trying hard to achieve perfect attendance all year. I thought I had it until three days before the end of the school year, when I came down with a nasty virus and a raging fever, rendering me too sick to attend.

However, these two things pale in comparison to when I was in fourth grade. I learned to read when I was four, so I excelled at reading. My teacher announced that in addition to the three reading groups she had established based on aptitude, she would be picking students to participate in an honors reading group for those that were at the top of the group. When she announced the names and my name did not appear, I was devastated! I went home and told my mother. Confused, she went to my teacher, who said she didn't think I was ready to enter a group like that. I couldn't believe she didn't recognize my potential.

Reflecting on those defining moments of my life, I think perhaps God was using them to humble me and allow me to rely on him. But because I didn't have a deep faith at that time, those moments instead made an indelible mark on my soul. Not only did my teacher not recognize my potential, I didn't either. I began to doubt my intelligence because of these "close, but no cigar" moments. When I wasn't excelling at school, it made the areas that I was not good at glaringly apparent. Now that I was afraid of performing poorly in subjects like reading and spelling, I dreaded going to gym, my worst subject.

The days of being humiliated in gym class are burned into my brain, as every week two captains were chosen to pick who would be on what team for whatever group sport we were playing. My friend and I always waited patiently as each captain whittled down the choices, and we would guess which one of us would be chosen last. More times than not, it was me.

Then one ordinary day, that changed. We lined up as we always did to be chosen for teams for that week's gym sport: dodgeball. The first captain made her first choice for her team, which was the most athletic classmate, as usual. I looked down at the floor, shuffling my shoes and admiring the white tennis shoes I had just purchased last week, when all of a sudden I heard my name. I looked up with a start. I motioned to myself in disbelief. The girl nodded as she confirmed she wanted me on her team. For once, someone had noticed me. For someone who had felt invisible her whole life, I basked in that few minutes of being wanted, noticed, desired. I knew she wasn't doing it because I had magically become a better athlete. She was doing it to show compassion to the ones who were always chosen last. In that moment, it didn't matter why she had chosen me; she just had.

Although that was many years go, that is still one of the highlights of my childhood. That day showed that God saw me for who I was, not for what I could do. In the last chapter, we talked about how works-based salvation and feeling obligated to work for our salvation can drive a wedge between us and God. Favoritism can also drive that wedge, because instead of feeling I could work to earn God's love, favoritism (or lack thereof) told me I was not worth being loved at all. Little did I know that all those events in elementary school skewed my view of God and his unconditional love for me. Because I wasn't favored, I saw myself as unlovable, unworthy, and of no value to God. These thoughts, although unspoken, affected how I saw my world and others. It was not until I attended a conference a couple of years ago that God revealed how much this was really affecting me.

In a time alone with God, I journaled all the times I felt I lost out on something, or the times when I worked so hard, only to fall short. This caused me to distrust God and believe the lie that God did not care about me. When I was able to release that anger and jealousy, I felt a heavy burden lifted from my shoulders. I was now able to live in freedom and take the first steps toward accepting God's unconditional love for me.

In his book *Soul Care*, Dr. Reimer expounds on the sin of favoritism through the story of Joseph and his brothers. He says,

> Joseph was greatly affected by the family sin of favoritism. It wasn't just that his brothers hated him. He developed an attitude of pride, and he struggled with comparing himself and others. This is typical of someone who has experienced the sin of favoritism in his or her upbringing. They are competitive and comparative; they are always seeking to establish their pecking order, fearful that their place in life will be lost.[2]

Many people struggled with the sin of favoritism. One of the more obvious examples in the Old Testament is that of Rachel and Leah:

> When the LORD saw that Leah was hated, he opened her womb, but Rachel was barren. And Leah conceived and bore a son, and she called his name Reuben, for she said, "Because the LORD has looked upon my affliction; for now my husband will love me."
>
> She conceived again and bore a son, and said, "Because the LORD has heard that I am hated, he has given me this son also." And she called his name Simeon.
>
> Again she conceived and bore a son, and said, "Now this time my husband will be attached to me, because I have borne him three sons." Therefore his name was called Levi.
>
> And she conceived again and bore a son, and said, "This time I will praise the LORD." Therefore she called his name Judah. Then she ceased bearing.

When Rachel saw that she bore Jacob no children, she envied her sister. She said to Jacob, "Give me children, or I shall die!"

Jacob's anger was kindled against Rachel, and he said, "Am I in the place of God, who has withheld from you the fruit of the womb?"

Then she said, "Here is my servant Bilhah; go in to her, so that she may give birth on my behalf, that even I may have children through her."

So she gave him her servant Bilhah as a wife, and Jacob went in to her. And Bilhah conceived and bore Jacob a son.

Then Rachel said, "God has judged me, and has also heard my voice and given me a son." Therefore she called his name Dan.

Rachel's servant Bilhah conceived again and bore Jacob a second son. Then Rachel said, "With mighty wrestlings I have wrestled with my sister and have prevailed." So she called his name Naphtali.

When Leah saw that she had ceased bearing children, she took her servant Zilpah and gave her to Jacob as a wife. Then Leah's servant Zilpah bore Jacob a son. And Leah said, "Good fortune has come!" so she called his name Gad.

Leah's servant Zilpah bore Jacob a second son. And Leah said, "Happy am I! For women have called me happy." So she called his name Asher.

In the days of wheat harvest Reuben went and found mandrakes in the field and brought them to his mother Leah. Then Rachel said to Leah, "Please give me some of your son's mandrakes."

> But she said to her, "Is it a small matter that you have taken away my husband? Would you take away my son's mandrakes also?" Rachel said, "Then he may lie with you tonight in exchange for your son's mandrakes."
>
> When Jacob came from the field in the evening, Leah went out to meet him and said, "You must come in to me, for I have hired you with my son's mandrakes."
>
> So he lay with her that night. And God listened to Leah, and she conceived and bore Jacob a fifth son. Leah said, "God has given me my wages because I gave my servant to my husband." So she called his name Issachar. (Gen. 29:31–30:18 ESV)

A few things to note about this passage:

Comparison leads to envy. Verse one in chapter 30 says, "When Rachel saw that she bore Jacob no children, she envied her sister." Rachel was not content with the great love she shared with her husband. She must have known that Jacob did not love Leah as much as her. Instead of enjoying the blessing of having her husband's affections and believing that was enough to satisfy her, she instead coveted what Leah had. Soon contentment gave way to entitlement. Not only should she have her husband's love, but also his children. His sin of favoritism led to her discontentment with who she was as a woman.

Envy gives way to greed. Did you see how fast Rachel and Leah went to war? Chapter 30 verses 1–3 say, "She said to Jacob, 'Give me children, or I shall die!' Jacob's anger was kindled against Rachel, and he said, 'Am I in the place of God, who has withheld from you the fruit of the womb?' Then she said, 'Here is my servant Bilhah; go in to her, so that she may give birth on my behalf, that even I may have children through her.'"

Sister pitted against sister, bearing children and showing them off as trophies rather than blessings. In that society, bearing children was what gave worth to women. To be barren meant they were not women at all, that they were less than the second-class citizens the world already told them they were. Their perspectives became skewed once Jacob approved of Leah when she bore him his first son.

Greed gives way to objectification. Soon, Jacob's love is not enough either. He becomes an object to use solely for procreation, not to enjoy the intimacy they shared. Chapter 30 verses 14 and 15 say, "In the days of wheat harvest Reuben went and found mandrakes in the field and brought them to his mother Leah. Then Rachel said to Leah, 'Please give me some of your son's mandrakes.' But she said to her, 'Is it a small matter that you have taken away my husband? Would you take away my son's mandrakes also?' Rachel said, 'Then he may lie with you tonight in exchange for your son's mandrakes.'"

Jacob becomes the target of what he can give and what he can do for them, not for who he is as a man. When we lust after the possessions of others, they become objects of personal gain, falsely boosting our self-esteem. Instead of placing their worship where it belonged, which was in God, and being grateful for what they had, they made other things the target of worship, building idols and reducing Jacob and the mandrakes God had blessed them with to *less than* rather than *good enough.*

Greed and favoritism are often linked. When someone who is favored constantly tries to attain his or her favored position in life, others often become casualties of greed in the process. As Rachel demonstrated, other people (namely Leah) are merely objects in a quest to earn others' love. Just like works-based salvation, favoritism is a sin that wedges its way between you and God. The eldest was the favorite because he was the firstborn son. But when the prodigal got away with getting his inheritance without doing any work, it must have devastated the eldest. Soon the prodigal was nothing more than a commodity to his older brother—not a human being to demonstrate compassion toward, but an object to be thrown away simply because he didn't meet his brother's expectations.

Comparison and the Eldest

The eldest also compared himself to the prodigal. Instead of rejoicing in the fact that he has followed the rules and made his father proud, the eldest compares himself to his brother, pointing out to his father that he is better.

Peter struggled with comparison, too. Most Christians remember Peter for his denial of Jesus before he was to be crucified. But John gives us a unique glimpse of Jesus's gracious reinstatement of Peter to his fellowship. Jesus asks Peter three times, "Do you love me?" Perplexed, Peter says yes. Jesus responds the same way every time: "Feed my sheep." Instead of being grateful for Jesus's grace in the face of his denial, he spots John walking behind him:

> Peter turned and saw that the disciple whom Jesus loved was following them. (This was the one who had leaned

> back against Jesus at the supper and had said, "Lord, who is going to betray you?") When Peter saw him, he asked, "Lord, what about him?" Jesus answered, "If I want him to remain alive until I return, what is that to you? You must follow me." Because of this, the rumor spread among the believers that this disciple would not die. But Jesus did not say that he would not die; he only said, "If I want him to remain alive until I return, what is that to you?" (John 21:20–23)

Like Rachel, Peter is jockeying for position, trying to get back in Jesus's good graces. Instead of recognizing the unconditional love and grace that Jesus is offering, he tries to knock down John while elevating himself. It's no coincidence that John refers to himself as the disciple whom Jesus loved several times in this same Gospel. Peter lost his chance to be aligned with Christ when he denied him. But John never denied Christ. He's the one who leaned on Jesus's bosom. He's the only one of the Twelve who watched Jesus's crucifixion. Peter, now trying to get back into Jesus's good graces, harbors jealousy and envy that could have caused a rift between them. But Jesus doesn't allow jealousy to reign. He extends grace in an effort to even the score between Peter and John. Jesus encourages Peter to be content even when the future seems uncertain.

Similarly, the father in the parable tries to level the playing field between the eldest and the prodigal. Jealousy rears its head when the eldest complains that he doesn't get a party. The father offers the eldest an invitation to be content and celebrate with them, allowing him a chance to release his jealousy.

Jennifer Dukes Lee, in her article *Curbing Comparison*, says,

> Someone always gets hurt when we compare, even if we think it's a secret battle we're fighting on the inside.

> It hurts us, and it hurts the person sitting on the other side of our envy. Comparison creates an us-versus-them mentality that can rob the body of Christ of its unity and fellowship. And it can open up doorways to petty criticism of the people we believe are "living in paradise."[3]

Underneath that comparison trap lurks a private yearning to be good enough, worthy enough, to be special and above all others. But what I fail to realize is that in all that wanting stands the One who already settled my worth a long time ago.

Second Corinthians 10:12 says, "But in all this comparing and grading and competing, they quite miss the point" (*The Message*). This sums it up, doesn't it? How often we miss out on the beauty of the presence of Jesus when we are too busy focusing on what's around us. This is nothing new. Many people in the Bible struggled with the sin of comparison. Cain compared himself to Abel, Jacob compared himself to Esau, and Rachel competed with Leah for Jacob's affections and for his offspring.

John 21:17–19 says,

> The third time he said to him, "Simon son of John, do you love me?" Peter was hurt because Jesus asked him the third time, "Do you love me?" He said, "Lord, you know all things; you know that I love you." Jesus said, "Feed my sheep. Very truly I tell you, when you were younger you dressed yourself and went where you wanted; but when you are old you will stretch out your hands, and someone else will dress you and lead you where you do not want to go." Jesus said this to indicate the kind of death by which Peter would glorify God. Then he said to him, "Follow me!"

Three interesting things about this passage:

1. **Peter robbed God of his glory and placed it on himself.** Instead of humbling himself, living in the reality of his recent betrayal, Peter focuses on what he isn't getting (an easy death) rather than seeing the situation for what it is: a chance to be reinstated to fellowship.
2. **Peter believed he loved God, but his actions proved otherwise.** It's no accident that in the paragraph before this, Jesus reinstates Peter to fellowship after his infamous denial by asking if he loved him. When Peter got frustrated and asked Jesus why he kept asking him if he loved him, Peter said he did. But feeding his sheep meant thinking of others before himself. It wasn't two seconds after he said he loved God that he didn't even think that in order to love God, he needed to love his apostles, whom he referred to as his "brothers."
3. **Peter chose to starve the sheep rather than feed them.** We can't be considered Christians if we don't love our brothers and sisters in Christ. To feed God's sheep means to provide for them physically, emotionally, and spiritually. A lack of love starves the sheep; it doesn't feed them.

You can, however, avoid the trap of comparison by following three principles:

1. **Replace entitlement with contentment.** Comparison means you feel you deserve the thing you want, when in reality, you haven't earned anything. God gives us all we have, and he can take it away at will. Be content with

what you have, not discontent with what you don't. Don't feel you deserve anything; rejoice that God gives you good gifts as he leads.

2. **Replace the lie of comparison with the truth of joy.** Once you have attained contentment, you will begin to have joy for all the ways God has blessed you. Satan wants to rob you of your joy, but don't let him. It helps when you stop looking at your joy and start looking to others.
3. **Place your eyes back on God, the One in front of you.** Peter took his eyes off Jesus when John walked by. There will always be people who will be prettier, thinner, smarter, faster, and a myriad of other things than us. But it's okay. Keep your eyes on the One in front of you, Jesus, without whose help we can do nothing.

If I'm honest, I may never stop wanting to look to others for approval. But if I keep my eyes on Jesus and off other people, I'll realize how blessed I am to be in his presence and not out trying to measure up to a system that is always broken.

DISCUSSION QUESTIONS

1 In what ways do you compare yourself to others? How does this practice hinder God's intention for wanting to free you from your Pharisaic tendencies?

2 Both Rachel and Peter missed an opportunity to worship God and trust in him wholly. What could they have done instead of comparing themselves to others in order to strengthen their relationship with God?

3 How does our media-saturated world contribute to the temptation to compare ourselves to others?

NOTES

[1]John E. Dubler, "Parable of the Prodigal Son: Part II, The Elder Brother" (n.p., n.d.), http://www.johndubler.com/Parables_27_WEB_Parable_of_the_Prodigal_Son_Part_II.pdf.

[2]Rob Reimer, *Soul Care: 7 Transformational Principles for a Healthy Soul* (Franklin, TN: Carpenter's Son Publishing, 2016).

[3]Jennifer Dukes Lee, "Curbing Comparison," *Today's Christian Woman*, April 2014, http://www.todayschristianwoman.com/articles/2014/april/curbing-comparison.html.

Chapter Eight

Never Disobeyed Your Orders

But he answered his father, "Look! All these years I've been slaving for you and never disobeyed your orders." (Luke 15:29)

Whatcha get? This was a common question I got asked in my elementary school classes. Because it was a small class and I went through each grade with the same girls, competition and comparison were familiar coats we wore each day. I wore them too. The security of having the best grade in the class offered me a comfortable yet temporary band-aid over my heart. Yet when I hadn't done well on a particular test, I'd cower in the corner, spewing a spiteful "I'm not telling" back at them. Every time I'd get a good grade, I'd wear my intelligence like a badge, parading it around for all to see.

It all came to a head, however, when at the end of my eighth-grade year, I expected all of my collective good grades would earn me the coveted position of salutatorian of my class. The day came when the principal made the long-awaited announcement. When she spoke into the microphone and announced someone else's name and not mine, I was devastated. The badge of intelligence had been stripped from me, leaving the deep wounds of insignificance and rejection exposed for all to see. I thought I was stroking my ego when I was parading my good grades around, but instead I was tearing others down in order to raise myself up.

I was a classic rule-follower. If there was a rule, I followed it. It started in elementary school, as the above story demonstrates, but even after graduation and when I became a Christian years later, my rule-following turned into a false sense of pride and arrogance where I judged others based on how closely they followed the rules. I've traded in good grades for a well-received article I've written, or I flaunt my kids' accomplishments on Facebook. I can stop rule-following in an effort to earn God's love, but until I deal with the root causes of comparison that lurk deep within my soul, I'll never be free.

The eldest struggled with this too. His declaration to his father that he has never disobeyed orders is like me, sitting in the front row of class, books neatly placed in the right-hand corner of my desk, assigned chapters read and highlighted, notes perfectly scrawled in an accompanying notebook. Hands folded on my desk, waiting for the teacher to arrive. This is how I spent my years in elementary school. I loved school, not just because I loved to learn but because it was the place where I felt like I was someone. I was good at school, and although I had to work hard to achieve my grades, I often made the honor roll, which gave me a sense of purpose.

Until I began a real relationship with Jesus, I found my worth in my intelligence. Once my life changed, I then found my worth in the purposes he had set out for me: making disciples, helping and healing those who need it. Before Christ, my worth was based on serving myself rather than others. Christ turned my purpose outward, showing me that true purpose means I have worth when I meet others' needs instead of my own.

In 2007, God called us to plant our first church. We expected that the first year would fluctuate in terms of attendance and finances. But little did we know that it would continue that way throughout the five years we kept the church open. We knew we had to make sacrifices, but the financial ones were the hardest. When the treasurer came to my husband and said the finances were not going as planned, my husband volunteered to take a pay cut. This meant I needed to take on more hours at a daycare to make ends meet and my husband had to take a second job. A few months later, the finances kept slipping, so he volunteered to take another pay cut. This increased our risk of losing our home. When the church met to discuss what we could do to help increase our income stream, my husband and I were shocked to learn that some members of the church had already been talking, and they all thought the best course of action was for my husband to stop taking a salary from the church and work full-time as a bi-vocational pastor, volunteering his time at the church. To say we were blindsided is an understatement. As I sat in silence as the church discussed our fate, a million thoughts ran through my mind, most of them a result of my feelings of hurt and betrayal. *How could they do this to me? After all I have done for them?*

The members entered our church with their own baggage, too. They had endured their own painful church experiences and came to us with bags in tow. But their preconceived notions about what church and the role of pastors should be were now affecting our lives. It wasn't until years after the church doors closed and we moved away that I was able to reconcile my feelings about that event. I can imagine that was what the eldest felt when the prodigal went against societal norms and squandered his money. Like the eldest, we had done everything we could, given the situation. We took second jobs, took pay cuts when necessary, and even got a permanent place to meet each Sunday after moving locations several times. Like the eldest, we did everything we thought God wanted us to do, and it wasn't enough.

The day of our last meeting, we watched as our most regular attenders gathered together one last time to say goodbye. I looked around the room and realized how much God had actually done, even though it didn't seem like it as we went through it. Through our labor, we met a bunch of great people, improved our community, and helped some people experience Jesus in a new way. It was hard to see what God had accomplished when I was close to my pain, but when I took a step back, I realized God had been present with us and had been doing his work right in front of us.

The eldest had trouble seeing all he had in front of him, too. Through every seed he planted and every weed he pulled, God was accomplishing his work through the eldest too, except he couldn't see it that way. Instead, he saw the father's gift of the inheritance as some sort of sick crime, and it was the eldest's job to balance the scales to ensure that justice was served. When he tells the father, "I've never disobeyed your orders," he's using his obedience as a kind of noose to wrap around the father's neck. In the eldest's mind, the father owes him his loyalty above the prodigal for as long as he lives.

ENVY AND THE ELDEST

Envy has been an enemy of mine for most of my life as a Christian. As someone who works hard and follows the rules, it is easy to see myself as the worker who didn't get what she deserves. More work deserves more pay, right? It's like Sally when she says in *A Charlie*

Brown Christmas as she makes out her Christmas list, "All I want is what I have coming to me. All I want is my fair share."

The latest experience I had with envy appeared as I spoke at a retreat for women. I knew the other two speakers' presentations were going to be lighthearted, exciting, and rich with opportunities for bonding and fellowship. But I knew what God had given me to say was going to bring about the necessary change the Holy Spirit wanted to initiate, the surgery needed to open people's hearts and extract the deep hurts and wounds keeping them from intimacy and true fellowship with God. Grousing and grumbling, I muttered in disgust, "Why do I always have to be the person that brings conviction and pain? Why can't I be the one that everyone likes?"

In that moment, the Spirit spoke to my heart: "It's because when I call you to do something, you say yes. I may be using them to bond them through fellowship, but it is through you and your willingness to be transparent, open, and vulnerable that I want to usher in my Spirit. Will you let me do that through you?" When I went to speak, the tears soon started to flow, and I was able to share a painful experience that was affecting my view of who God was and his role in my life. Through my vulnerability, more people began to share their difficult experiences that were keeping them from experiencing God in a deep way. The tears flowed, and so did the vulnerability. As I wiped my tears away, I realized that if I had continued complaining or even refused to be used by God in such a way, I would have missed an opportunity to commune with Jesus. The eldest spent so much time complaining, navel gazing, and reflecting on all he had lost that he forgot to count on what he was gaining—an invitation to cultivate the land for the kingdom and to be used by God for his purposes and in the way in which he saw fit.

In the days after the retreat, I realized something: I was focused on the wrong thing. Instead of boasting in the joy that comes from surrender and being an empty vessel, I pouted and fretted over how I was seen in others' eyes. Hard work is always rewarded—just not always in the way we think or want it to be. Consider this passage in Matthew 25:14–27:

> Again, it will be like a man going on a journey, who called his servants and entrusted his wealth to them. To one he gave five bags of gold, to another two bags, and to another one bag, each according to his ability. Then he went on his journey. The man who had received five bags of gold went at once and put his money to work and gained five bags more. So also, the one with two bags of gold gained two more. But the man who had received one bag went off, dug a hole in the ground and hid his master's money.
>
> After a long time the master of those servants returned and settled accounts with them. The man who had received five bags of gold brought the other five. "Master," he said, "you entrusted me with five bags of gold. See, I have gained five more."
>
> His master replied, "Well done, good and faithful servant! You have been faithful with a few things; I will put you in charge of many things. Come and share your master's happiness!"
>
> The man with two bags of gold also came. "Master," he said, "you entrusted me with two bags of gold; see, I have gained two more."
>
> His master replied, "Well done, good and faithful servant! You have been faithful with a few things; I will put you in charge of many things. Come and share your master's happiness!"

> Then the man who had received one bag of gold came. "Master," he said, "I knew that you are a hard man, harvesting where you have not sown and gathering where you have not scattered seed. So I was afraid and went out and hid your gold in the ground. See, here is what belongs to you."
>
> His master replied, "You wicked, lazy servant! So you knew that I harvest where I have not sown and gather where I have not scattered seed? Well then, you should have put my money on deposit with the bankers, so that when I returned I would have received it back with interest."

A treasure such as an opportunity to grow deeper in the faith can't be buried and hidden, or else it won't reap a reward. The treasure to relish the growth that took place could have only been achieved through pruning. Someone who has the boldness to cut off dead branches gets to enjoy the growth that takes place because the tree's deadness is no longer holding it back. God was giving me a gift that I almost threw away. I was so interested in following the rules so that society would respect me that I had forgotten God longed to have fellowship with me in ways that went much deeper than just an obligatory maintenance of the land. He wanted me not just to sweep the surface of the retreat attenders' hearts but to get down to the root, digging deeper until the sin that was causing them deadness could be exposed. Like a potter with clay, he wanted to dig, pulling the sin from its roots and exposing the raw earth underneath. Not only that, but he wanted me to water that new land, placing deep within it the seeds that contained everything it needed for growth in Christ to flourish. If he had chosen me to be the lighthearted, funny speaker, it would have been a great time, but no growth would have taken place. My willingness to expose the wounded, sin-stained parts of my soul allowed others to follow suit. As a good tender of the land, the eldest had the same opportunity. But he became so focused on the rules of thc land and his dictated role in the family that he forgot to be the lover of souls, teaching the youngest brother that a sin-stained soul is no path to freedom. Instead, a heart willing to restrain its rebellion is the path to true growth and life.

If only the eldest understood that his heart of rebellion needed to be restrained a bit, too.

We all want life to work. We all want a magic formula that, when calculated and executed, makes life go according to plan. Larry Crabb, in his book *The Pressure's Off*, speaks about this as he shares a story of a woman who questions what she is doing wrong when life has not gone as planned:

> "What am I doing wrong?" The question was never far from the woman's mind. Tonight it screamed from the deep places within her, demanding the answer that never came.
>
> "Look at my life. Things aren't turning out as I had hoped. Why don't I feel better about myself? Why is life sometimes so difficult? I must be doing something terribly wrong."
>
> The woman did not believe she was being punished for wrongdoing by a vengeful deity, although that thought was sometimes hard to resist. She did, however, believe there was a right way to live that would make her life work. Of course there was. But she could not find the way. . . .

> [Then a Voice spoke to her:] "Your desires are too weak. Small affections create idols, unworthy gods to whom you sacrifice your life. Your prayers are idol worship. You've been bound to your desire for the Better Life, which you define by your experience of pleasure and pain. I've come to show you the New Way that leads to the Better Hope."[1]

The old way points to the easy road, one lined with prosperity and abundance and luxury. The other, the new way, which God wants for us, rockier on the surface, is lined with difficulties, trials, and tribulations. For many, this would be an easy choice. Skip down the road paved with ease and thank yourself for a life on Easy Street.

Which would you choose?

Would you go for the easier road? The easy road is available to you now. All you have to do is put on your false self, put on your pretentions, cover up your flaws, and plaster on your fake smile.

Would you do it? Would you take the easy road like others, or would you willingly choose the road racked with pain if you knew you could be free?

That is what the Lord is offering you today. He is asking you to take the road less traveled. He wants you to adopt a new way of living, one that doesn't seek to fulfill its own desires but that seeks to put others first. This road, although difficult, can lead you to a place of love, of worth, of freedom. He wants you to walk, even limp, taking one step at a time down the road he has made for you. It won't be easy; nothing in life ever is. But the rockier road has something the easier, paved road does not: a Lord who wants to walk beside you. Just as Jesus walked the rocky road with Peter toward repentance, so are you called to walk that same rocky road.

You will stumble along the way; everyone does. When you fall, a steady hand will be available to help you stand on your feet. The Lord will help you dust yourself off and walk again. At times he might have to carry you, when your tired and weary bones will no longer let you put one foot in front of the other. No matter how difficult the road gets, you will always have someone that will help you get there.

Now that makes the road worth walking.

You can walk that road today. It starts with ridding yourself of envy and comparison, letting your flaws show and becoming fully exposed (no matter how raw that might be) before the Lord. It means wiping the tears away, dusting yourself off, and taking baby steps down the long, rocky road. It's rough, but it's beautiful. Adam and Eve had the opportunity to repair their severed connection with God. But they chose not to take it. They took the paved road, too. They walked down it hand in hand, but they fell a few times. They wished they had someone to help them up, but they didn't. It was easier, but it was lonely.

God is giving you the same opportunity to repair your relationship with him and fill your need for deep knowledge and connection. You have the chance to take the road less traveled.

Will you take it?

That's my prayer for you, dear reader, as God continues to reveal to you his intention for a new way for you. God intends for you to find a new way of living a life where you enjoy the pleasure of accepting an invitation to receive everything the father has for you, rather than grumbling out in the field. The new way is out there. A better life is within your grasp. It is your choice whether or not you will reach for it, take the Father's hand, and join the feast.

DISCUSSION QUESTIONS

1 Have you ever struggled with envy? Name a time in your life when envy has crept into your life and reared its ugly head. How did you resolve it?

2 The parable of the workers is obviously a parallel of God and his offer of salvation to all. Which workers can you relate to the most: The workers who worked all day, or the ones who worked less but got paid the same? Have you ever resented working more than someone else? Why or why not?

3 Do you relate to the story of the woman who wants to live a better life? How did you feel when the voice told her she needed to live a new way and abandon her old way of praying and thinking? In what ways can you resign your old way of obtaining pleasure and avoiding pain and adopt the new way, abundant with highs and lows?

NOTE

[1]Larry Crabb, The Pressure's Off (Colorado Springs: Waterbrook Press, 2002), 3, 6.

Chapter Nine

Yet You Never Gave Me Even a Young Goat

Yet you never gave me even a young goat
so I could celebrate with my friends. (Luke 15:29)

I've been in ministry sixteen years, and I've seen many ups and downs during that time. I've had the privilege of sitting beside a church member as he held his dying wife's hand as she passed from life into Jesus's arms. I've grabbed towels from home and watched from the back of the sanctuary as person after person arose from their seat in the congregation and agreed to be baptized after two scheduled baptisms took place. Those are the moments I will remember forever.

Then there are not-so-good times.

I remember when we set off to our next church destination, leaving behind a disgruntled church. I remember my husband inserting the key and closing down the church plant we had worked so hard to build. I also remember looking over my shoulder in the rearview mirror as we drove away from our home we lost because we could no longer afford it.

Closing down our church plant was one of the most difficult times in my life—difficult for my marriage as well as my emotional, mental, and physical well-being. I was working at a job I hated when I wanted to be home writing, my husband had to take a second job when pay cuts due to low attendance threatened to take our home, and I was mad at God.

Being mad at God always comes back to haunt you.

Although I didn't realize it at the time, my anger was keeping me from communing with God. Little by little, that anger was tearing away at my soul, robbing me of the peace and joy afforded me through the promises of Christ. Instead, one worrisome thought crept into my mind. Since I hadn't taken it captive and replaced it with the truth, that thought turned into two, then three, then too many to count, until they came too naturally to ignore. Soon my anger took root, and bitterness and resentment emerged. This colored my view of everything and everyone. Soon I couldn't enter my new church door without having a bad attitude. I had created a monster, and only I could tame it.

As I came to God and analyzed what was bothering me, it was not the loss of our home or our church (although those losses contributed to my pain). It was the abandonment issues from years before that I had not resolved. As I mentioned earlier, when I was eighteen years old, I converted from Catholicism and became a born-again Christian. It was one of the best moments of my life, but my parents were not pleased. The news led to us fighting and long periods of not talking. When Thanksgiving came and no invitation to dinner came my way, I went to eat with my boyfriend and his family. The following Saturday, my parents came to my workplace and told me I was no longer welcome in their home. When

I got to my home, I found that all my belongings had been packed in black garbage bags and left in the garage. When I got there, my father loaded my bags in the back of his truck. He drove me to my boyfriend's home and told me they were my family now, and I was no longer living with him and my mom. Although God provided for me in ways I had never imagined, it took me a long time to finally resolve the emotional scars from that event.

In an earlier chapter, I also shared about my relationship with my sister. Little did I know that those issues of feeling like I needed to earn my mother's approval never left me. What I realized was that someone doesn't have to leave you to create issues of abandonment. Those feelings of being unloved spilled into my adulthood, and into my relationships with everyone I knew and loved. However, God, in his infinite wisdom, lovingly showed me that he would never leave or forsake me. Once I was able to understand and walk in the light of this truth, I was able to work through my feelings of abandonment and let go of all that anger and replace it with unswerving joy, an undeniable sense of peace, and the unconditional love of my Father. God yearned to fulfill roles of both mother and father to me. In so doing, I was able to live in freedom, unbound by the chains of abandonment and loss.

This is the crossroads the eldest son faced, too. Angered by the father's sudden display of hospitality to the prodigal, the eldest complains that his father never showed him the appreciation he felt he deserved. This anger over what he believed he did not receive gave way to bitterness and allowed resentment to take root. Now the eldest stands at the door, unable to let himself go in and enjoy the feast. His father, pleading with him to come, offers him the appreciation he desires, "'My son,' the father said, 'you are always with me, and everything I have is yours'" (verse 31). His ingratitude, much like the prodigal's ingratitude for all that the father gave him in terms of the property and the inheritance, plagued his soul. His anger and feelings of seeming abandonment darkened his soul too. All he has to do is accept the invitation.

This isn't the last time we see this image of opening the door of our hearts to Jesus. Jesus offers all of us the same opportunity to open the door and eat with him in Revelation 3:20: "Here I am! I stand at the door and knock. If anyone hears my voice and opens the door, I will come in and eat with that person, and they with me." Jesus extends the same open-ended invitation to you and me as the father in the parable extends to the eldest. All we have to do is accept.

THE DISEASE OF INGRATITUDE

What strikes me about the eldest's statement about the father not even giving him a goat is that it's a bit shocking. Didn't his father just "divide the inheritance between them"? The father could have only given the inheritance to the prodigal and made the eldest wait, as was the custom at the time. But instead, he gives the eldest his inheritance now, relieving him of his responsibility to take care of him when he dies. He had plenty of money to celebrate with his friends. After all, the prodigal demonstrates he can do just that. But his statement packs more of a punch, going straight to the father's gut. He's not just asking for money; he's asking for love.

As parents, we do the best we can for our children. We work hard, providing their basic needs; and if we are lucky, we can afford to indulge some of their desire for material possessions as well. I can imagine that the father (who we know is a parallel to our heavenly Father) does the same for us. He provides us with everything we need to survive. Sometimes he allows us the desires of our hearts as well.

Just as the eldest doubted the father's love for him, so did the people in the book of Malachi doubt the Father's love. Malachi 1:2–3 says,

> "I have loved you," says the LORD. "But you ask, 'How have you loved us?' Was not Esau Jacob's brother?" declares the LORD. "Yet I have loved Jacob, but Esau I have hated, and I have turned his hill country into a wasteland and left his inheritance to the desert jackals."

"How have you loved us?" must have grieved the Father's heart. If Israel had said that to me, I would have shouted from the rooftops, "How can you be so selfish? After all I've done for you!" Yet God, demonstrating again his unending grace and love, sheds light on his love for them:

> But this is what the LORD Almighty says: "They may build, but I will demolish. They will be called the Wicked Land, a people always under the wrath of the LORD. You will see it with your own eyes and say, 'Great is the LORD—even beyond the borders of Israel!'" (verses 4–5)

It is so like us as Christians to blame God when circumstances in our lives don't go as planned. It is also easy for us to think we are doing better than we are in our spiritual lives. Yet, if we examine our lives through God's lens, we quickly see that the reputations we consider blameless are actually full of holes, like a thin slice of Swiss cheese. In this passage, God quickly points out that the people of Israel were giving him flawed or less than perfect sacrifices as their offering. The leaders, in turn, were allowing it, instead of telling the people that the sacrifices were blemished! Instead of praising God for his mercy on them for giving him less than their best, they complained.

It's the same for the eldest brother. The fact that he was complaining to his father that he had not even given him a young goat means he doesn't even recognize the father's provisions for him. In fact, he not only insults the prodigal by calling him "this son of yours," but he takes it one step further and insults the father, too! Normally, people would bring a fatted calf if they were going to offer something of worth to God. To ask for just a young goat is like saying, "You haven't done anything for me!" He takes all God has done for granted because the offering was not as flashy as what the father was giving the prodigal. As God does with Israel, the father gently reminds the eldest that he has provided for him and rewarded him for his work when he says, "Everything I have is yours."

As fellow Pharisees, we resort to complaining instead of praising God for his provision. When situations turn from good to bad or God does not answer our prayers in a timely fashion, we morph into babies stomping our feet and cursing the sky instead of being grateful for all that God has done. We also get angry with God when he doesn't do the one thing we want him to do, instead of focusing on all the other things he has done.

The disease of ingratitude has invaded the older brother's heart, seeping into every nook and cranny, until all that is left is anger and resentment. As Luke reminds us just a few chapters before, "A good man brings good things out of the good stored up in his heart, and an evil man brings evil things out of the evil stored up in his heart. For the mouth speaks what the heart is full of" (Luke 6:45). The eldest probably stored up this resentment for a long time. Whether he felt this way before the prodigal left on his wild spree or during the time they waited for his return (the Bible gives us no indication of how long it takes for him to return), it is apparent the eldest felt this way about how his father treats him versus how he treats his brother for a while; otherwise, he would not have spewed his venom so quickly.

What was he expecting? Was it really a party he was looking for or merely a little nod in his direction or a pat on the back for a job well done? As is the case with many people, the father's approval was worth more than any inheritance to the eldest son. As was the custom, the eldest received the blessing, and as we discussed before, he would have received double, so why wasn't that enough? He obviously felt unappreciated, unwanted, and unloved to settle for just a young goat. The disease of ingratitude had burrowed deep into his soul, breeding an infestation of lies and bitterness. Nothing would be good enough for him. It didn't matter if the father had said, "Everything is yours"; it was never going to be enough.

At a conference held by my district, one event they conduct at the end is a father blessing. For members that want to participate, the pastors lay hands on the participants and speak words of encouragement and love over them. Soliciting help from the Holy Spirit, they speak as though God the Father is speaking to them. In that moment, they get to hear the love and affection they feel they've never received from the father. My husband was able to participate and felt the presence of the Holy Spirit come upon him. He was able to let go of his feelings of failure when the church plant closed and was able to accept his heavenly Father's love. No longer did he seek the approval of family or friends, but sought God's approval instead.

Lysa TerKeurst said in her book *Uninvited,*

> Indeed, the world entices your flesh but never embraces your soul. All the while, the only love caring enough to embrace us and complete enough to fill us, waits. He waits every day with every answer we need, every

> comfort we crave, every affection we're desperate for, while we look everywhere but at Him. We run at a breakneck pace to try and achieve what God wants us to slow down enough to receive. He really does have it all worked out. The gaps are filled. The heartache is eased. The provision is ready. The needs are met. The questions are answered. The problems are solved. Live from the abundant place that you are loved, and you won't find yourself begging others for scraps of love.[1]

Just as the father waited for the prodigal son, he waits for the eldest, too, with arms open wide reassuring us, "Everything I have is yours."

It's clear that the father expressed just as much grace to the eldest son as he did to the youngest son. The prodigal, not deserving of his father's forgiveness, grace, and hospitality, is overwhelmed by the love the father demonstrates. Unlike the eldest, he accepts his father's love. The eldest, however, broods and complains, dismissing any of the father's blessings up to this point. But the eldest is also guilty of a different and equally dangerous sin—the sin of entitlement. He thinks he deserves all he has received and more, although his brother lives in the reality that he deserves nothing. Little does the eldest know, he doesn't deserve his blessings. He is given them simply because his father is generous.

M. Craig Barnes writes,

> I remind them, as the father does in the parable, that they already have all they ever wanted out of life. They readily agree that everything truly important to them has come by grace and not through their hard work. But I have to remember not to leverage their gratitude by saying, "Get back in the fields of hard work." The invitation of the father is for his elder son to come to the celebration. . . .

> Scripture makes it clear that repentance is a necessary response to the salvation of Jesus Christ. But of what do the righteous repent? Sin is anything that keeps us from God. So as odd as it sounds, the elder brother has to repent of the righteousness that is keeping him from needing Jesus. But it is much harder to repent of being good.[2]

Repent of righteousness? Is that even possible? I think it is. It really is at the center of my biggest heart issues in my relationship with the Lord. I am most resentful of him when I have done right and didn't get what I thought I deserved, and when I watch a "sinner" give a platitude to God and receive the same amount of grace that I receive. I followed the rules! I did what I was asked, and this other person didn't!

When we closed the doors on that church plant in 2012, I could have ticked it off in my mind as a silent grudge against God. I could have harbored bitterness or resentment as payback for the injustice I felt. But I didn't do either of those things. Instead, I searched my heart. I found the offensive ways and got rid of them. I forgave myself for feeling like it was our fault it had failed. I forgave God for his seeming lack of care or compassion. Lastly, I trusted that what God had done during those years was not in vain.

The eldest is not a bad person. As I mentioned in Chapter Two, he has a lot of good qualities. He is hardworking, as indicated by the fact that he still stays to care for the property even when he had received his reward. He is passionate, because he expresses to his father his feelings and that his treatment of his brother is unfair. He can be trusted if his father was willing to give him everything, including the double portion of his inheritance. Just like the Pharisees, he is an intelligent, strong leader, capable of maintaining and managing his father's assets. Just like the prodigal, the father loves him, too. Just as he has a place in the kingdom, so do the Pharisees. Jesus tells this parable in the presence of the Pharisees because he believes there is still hope for them, too. He doesn't dismiss them or their spiritual plight. He treats them as he would the poor and hopeless around him. He appeals to their intellect, since they were experts in the Law. His stories appealed to the common folk as they did to the Pharisees, and he wants both the Pharisee and common person to know his Father.

DISCUSSION QUESTIONS

1 Have you ever compared your behavior to that of a Pharisee? What have you learned about yourself?

2 Have you ever felt underappreciated by others for what you do? How do you think this relates to the eldest brother's words to his father?

3 When have you been ungrateful for what your heavenly Father has given you? What did you do (if anything) to change your attitude?

NOTES

[1]Lysa TerKeurst, *Uninvited* (Nashville: Thomas Nelson, 2016), 21.

[2]M. Craig Barnes, "The Prodigal's Brother," *The Christian Century* 129, no. 6 (2012): 35. ATLASerials, Religion Collection, EBSCOhost (accessed October 23, 2016).

Chapter Ten

I am Always with You

In the past few chapters we have uncovered the eldest son's deep-seated jealousy and envy of his brother, his ungratefulness and greed, and his holding the prodigal's deeds over his head rather than acting in love and grace. It seems I have been hard on the eldest, unmerciful in my assessment of his actions, and hesitant to believe he would accept the father's invitation to salvation. Yet, underneath all that baggage was a scared boy, looking for affirmation from his father, an affirmation he'd always had but never fully grasped. Because although Jesus intended to show the Pharisees listening from afar that he knew all about their hypocrisy, he also offered them hope. Just as Martha had hope and Peter could be restored to fellowship with Jesus, we too can throw off our false selves and become the people whom God can enjoy in an intimate relationship.

There is a tension we experience throughout our lives, like a devil and an angel who sit on our shoulders and talk us into making good or bad choices based solely on free will. In the eldest son's case, the devil was screaming lies into his ears, like "Everyone thinks you are a joke. Your brother doesn't care at all about you or your family name."

But the Lord waits for us. It is interesting to note that the father didn't run after the prodigal son. He only comes to him when he is repentant—when he has done the work of wanting to ask for forgiveness. Patience is the best strategy in this case, because even the father knows that a person can't allow the Spirit to work if their heart isn't ready. Although the prodigal needed to hit rock bottom before he would come to repentance, a story like Jesus's encounter with the woman at the well demonstrates her heart was ready, and God's waiting for her at the well turns into an opportunity for the woman to receive salvation. Let's consider the story for a moment:

> Now he had to go through Samaria. So he came to a town in Samaria called Sychar, near the plot of ground Jacob had given to his son Joseph. Jacob's well was there, and Jesus, tired as he was from the journey, sat down by the well. It was about noon.
>
> When a Samaritan woman came to draw water, Jesus said to her, "Will you give me a drink?" (His disciples had gone into the town to buy food.)
>
> The Samaritan woman said to him, "You are a Jew and I am a Samaritan woman. How can you ask me for a drink?" (For Jews do not associate with Samaritans.)
>
> Jesus answered her, "If you knew the gift of God and who it is that asks you for a drink, you would have asked him and he would have given you living water."

"Sir," the woman said, "you have nothing to draw with and the well is deep. Where can you get this living water? Are you greater than our father Jacob, who gave us the well and drank from it himself, as did also his sons and his livestock?"

Jesus answered, "Everyone who drinks this water will be thirsty again, but whoever drinks the water I give them will never thirst. Indeed, the water I give them will become in them a spring of water welling up to eternal life."

The woman said to him, "Sir, give me this water so that I won't get thirsty and have to keep coming here to draw water."

He told her, "Go, call your husband and come back."

"I have no husband," she replied.

Jesus said to her, "You are right when you say you have no husband. The fact is, you have had five husbands, and the man you now have is not your husband. What you have just said is quite true."

"Sir," the woman said, "I can see that you are a prophet. Our ancestors worshiped on this mountain, but you Jews claim that the place where we must worship is in Jerusalem."

"Woman," Jesus replied, "believe me, a time is coming when you will worship the Father neither on this mountain nor in Jerusalem. You Samaritans worship what you do not know; we worship what we do know, for salvation is from the Jews. Yet a time is coming and has now come when the true worshipers will worship the Father in the Spirit and in truth, for they are the kind of worshipers the Father seeks. God is spirit, and his worshipers must worship in the Spirit and in truth."

> The woman said, "I know that Messiah" (called Christ) "is coming. When he comes, he will explain everything to us."
>
> Then Jesus declared, "I, the one speaking to you—I am he." (John 4:4–26)

Here are a few things to note from this passage:

1. **The woman at the well wanted to be seen, too.** I know you could argue the opposite: she didn't want to be seen. But I don't mean physically. She was going to the well at an hour when she knew the town would not be there. She didn't want to have to deal with the whispers and the stares and the snickers behind her back. Yet Jesus, knowing she would be there, purposely stops at that well at that particular time just for her. By the end of the encounter, she rejoices not only in the offer of salvation, but also in the fact that God saw her as important, loved, and cherished. When we live in the reality that God loves us for who we are, waits for us, and desires fellowship with us, we don't have to look to others for their attention; we already have the King's attention! Jesus waited at that well. He waited for the Samaritan woman. He waits for me. He waits for you. He had the answers that would allow that woman to leave the well with more than just a simple jug of water, but with living water that allows us to never thirst again when we drink from it.
2. **Although the woman at the well is not specifically named, God knew who she was.** Even Mary Magdalene, known in her society as being lower class because she was a prostitute, had a name. So the fact that the woman here has no name probably means she was looked down

upon in her town. He searches for her, pursues her, and finds her. He communicates clearly that he knows who she is.

3. **She came to the well broken, but left feeling full.** She thinks she is going to get ordinary water from the well so she can temporarily quench her thirst. But Jesus didn't care as much about her physical thirst as he did her spiritual thirst. It is interesting that even after he says these words, she still doesn't understand the reality of who he is. She still asks for this water, meaning the water from the well. He asks her to call her husband so he can reveal to her who he truly is, but also so she won't use a man to quench her spiritual thirst, that void inside of her.

   Haven't we all used physical water to quench our spiritual thirst? This water could be anything—work, food, alcohol, drugs, sex, love, etc. Jesus is sitting at the well looking for you today. He wants to quench the deep spiritual thirst you have, too. Perhaps the reason the woman is not named is so that we can easily substitute any of our names and have it be just as relevant. Right? Haven't we all used some person's affection to fill the void that can only be filled by God? Before, she knew *of* him, but after meeting him face-to-face, she is transformed *by* him. She goes from hiding from the world to shouting from the rooftops who he is: "Come see a man who told me everything I ever did."

4. **He uses her past to impact the future.** He doesn't tell her about her past to shame her; quite the opposite. He tells her so she can get real with him. It is only through revelation from God that we can be transformed. That comes in many forms: his Word, prayer, other brothers

and sisters in Christ. Perhaps you think that God can't use you, that your past is too terrible to warrant use in the kingdom.

Here are some things the woman at the well does so she can find freedom in Christ, and which you can do too:

- **Redefine your past**—Come to grips with what you have done. If you have a shady past, accept it. There's nothing you can do to change it, so why dwell on it? What in your past (your story) is holding you back from being seen by the world, or from shouting from the rooftops about who God is?
- **Confess your sins**—It is only through repentance and acceptance of what we have done that God can use us. We can't live in the light as 1 John 1:7 says if we haven't brought out into the light what we have done. Confess it to someone. Satan is disarmed when we bring our sins out of hiding. Jesus disarmed the woman when he told her those sins, and he can do the same for us. He knows our sins; he just wants us to acknowledge them.
- **Let the transformative work God does in your life allow you to impact the kingdom**—Once you feel like you are free from all that baggage weighing you down, what is stopping you from doing his work? What might God be calling you to do now that you're free? Everyone has a purpose; we just need to find out what it is and not run from it, but do it.

The eldest needs to redefine his life. Instead of seeing his life as a letdown, full of rejection and disappointment, he could focus on what he actually has. He now has a double inheritance, beautiful land, and an intact reputation. The woman at the well didn't have any of this. She had a reputation of being a whore; she had no man to protect her or even meet her needs. Yet Jesus pursues her and sits and waits so he can be the man she has wanted her whole life.

Jesus extended the same invitation to the eldest brother that he did to the woman at the well. Jesus leaves the parable open-ended so that the crowd listening, the Pharisees, and even the future readers might take that invitation to drink from the well of living water, too.

Jesus offered the woman at the well not only salvation, but also fellowship with the Savior who was going to fill that deep void in her life. The eldest has a deep void in his life, too, although it is a bit more difficult to detect. He was looking for a man to validate who he was, too. The father, who has already offered the eldest everything he owns, now offers him the chance for wholeness.

Throughout this book, I have talked about my relationship with my sister, the oldest in our family. In a sense, I have acted as the oldest in the family, careful to follow every rule and cover up all family sins so that the family name can be preserved. With that comes a pressure to be more grown-up and keep the family together, even when the other sibling doesn't take it as seriously. My sister and I are four-and-a-half years apart in age. This didn't seem like an issue when we were young, as we spent numerous times playing Barbies and listening to records. But when she was high school age, I was nine-and-a-half, a gap too wide to fill with Barbies and fashion shows. When she went off to high school, I was left home to play alone, so I got used to entertaining myself. When she went to college and I was in high school, the gap became so wide that we never reconnected after that point. By this time, I was used to being alone, and my sister had established friends, made a home for herself in a college far away, and had gotten used to not being with me. When I became a Christian, we were even further divided. Growing up Catholic, I went to church every week. But my sister stopped going when she was in her early teens. While my thirst for Christ grew, her thirst was quenched by the busyness of life. Not only that, but I can hardly ignore the spiritual warfare that comes when someone dedicates their life to God:

> Do you think I came to bring peace on earth? No, I tell you, but division. From now on there will be five in one family divided against each other, three against two and two against three. They will be divided, father against son and son against father, mother against daughter and daughter against mother, mother-in-law against daughter-in-law and daughter-in-law against mother-in-law. (Luke 12:51–53)

Division always comes when someone begins to know God more intimately, and the prodigal and his brother are no different. No wonder the eldest felt threatened by the prodigal's pass from family responsibility and then his understanding of the father's love in a new way. Jan Riehl Orndorff writes,

> And if we think about it, most of us are really like the older brother. We accepted Jesus at a young age. We have worked hard all of our lives. We have tried to live right, follow the rules, be good Christians, treat others the way we should, and on, and on, and on. And it really is hard to see how some people are rewarded when they don't follow the rules. For example, the welfare mother who can't take care of the children she already has yet who is pregnant again, while a dedicated Christian couple struggles with infertility. Or the man who lies

> and cheats yet has a business that thrives, while the good Christian who follows fair business principles struggles to keep the business going. Or the old stooge who drinks like a fish and smokes a pack a day yet who lives to be ninety-five, while the Christian who has never touched the stuff dies of emphysema at the age of fifty-eight. It is hard not to get jealous when people seem to be getting away with so much while we try so hard to do what is right.[1]

Just as my sister and I got older and our interests changed and we withdrew from each other, so did the prodigal and the eldest. I can't imagine that the older brother, the rule-following personality, would have allowed his heart and mind to wander to rebelling against the father and his rules. When the younger brother rebelled, the older brother probably felt like he didn't have anything in common with the prodigal, widening that gap between brothers. When the prodigal comes back and is welcomed as if nothing has happened, when the rule-breaker becomes the favorite one, the divide widened so much that it was probably impossible to close it. Much like my sister and me, once our interests changed and I bound my heart to Jesus, we no longer had anything in common, and that separated us further. This divide still remains to this day.

Repentance Is the Key to Loving Relationships

What if, rather than the father doing so, the prodigal had come out to the older brother? Would that have changed the eldest brother's mind about joining the feast? What if the prodigal had that conversation that could have repaired it all? He could have said something like, "Brother, I'm sorry I wasn't there for you when you needed me. I've made a mess of things and satisfied my hedonistic pleasures rather than exhibiting the same loyalty to Dad as you did. I hope I can make it up to you some day, but I know it won't get better overnight. Can we start fresh and wipe the slate clean? Can you forgive me for all I've done? Come on, come into the party and let's toast to this new life—you and I taking care of all that Dad worked so hard to attain. What do you say?"

I can relate to this. Although I would love to reconcile with my sister, I know that if I simply sweep my feelings of hurt and disappointment under the rug and don't hold her accountable for her actions, we will just go back to the way things were before. It is interesting to note that yes, the father embarrasses himself in front of his son and society to welcome his wayward son home, but he doesn't welcome the son home until he is repentant. Our Father knows that even with the best of intentions, it is common for us to revert to our old ways of doing things, especially when a rebellious heart is tearing us away from the commitment we made to the Savior. Repentance is the key to real life change. We can't just say we want it; we have to mean it. Until my sister desires to have a different type of relationship with me, it would not be loving or helpful to me to let her back into my life. I would only be communicating the message that "your lack of respect not only for my feelings but also for our relationship as sisters would drive a wedge into the loving relationship we could have with each other."

The prodigal demonstrated repentance, but only to the father. Then he goes in to the party without a word to the brother. Repentance says to the offended party, "I'm not just going to say I'm sorry; I'm going to do something about it." In order to have loving relationships with others, we simply can't sin against others over and over and expect the blood of Christ to cover it. To do this is to make a mockery of what Christ did on the cross. Repentance is the public step necessary to turn words into actions.

DISCUSSION QUESTIONS

1 Jan Riehl Orndorff wrote, "And if we think about it, most of us are really like the older brother. We accepted Jesus at a young age. We have worked hard all of our lives. We have tried to live right, follow the rules, be good Christians, treat others the way we should, and on, and on, and on. And it really is hard to see how some people are rewarded when they don't follow the rules." What do you think about this statement? Do you see yourself in this statement? Why or why not?

2 Do you focus on what you do have or what you don't have? How does this relate to the behavior of the eldest brother?

3 Why do you think repentance is the key to having loving, successful relationships? Are there other characteristics a loving relationship should have as well?

NOTE

[1]Jan Riehl Orndorff, "What about the Older Brother?" in *Brethren Life and Thought* 50, no. 1–2 (2005): 43–47, accessed October 23, 2016.

Chapter Eleven

Everything I Have Is Yours

"Nana, do you know how to dance?" At age seven, I longed to glide gracefully across a dance floor and envisioned myself doing so in a long, flowing dress.

She chuckled to herself and answered, "We moved a little differently than you kids do today, but all dancing begins with a few basic steps."

"Can you show me? Please?"

I knew Nana, one of the most important people in my life, would never refuse my request. Because she lived in the adjacent house, I spent more time with her than just about anyone. I fondly remember going over to her house to have dinner on Sunday evenings. When Nana strolled into the kitchen, I lifted the lid and inhaled the steam from the garlic-infused potatoes and peered into the oven to watch the moist droplets of roast beef drip into the underlying pan.

During the summer, I would sleep over at Nana's. I remember packing my things, tucking a box of Frosted Flakes cereal under my arm, and making the trip next door. I loved spending my weekends there, watching while Nana finished her crossword puzzle at the kitchen table. Occasionally, we rocked slowly back and forth in matching rocking chairs as we enjoyed the cool breeze of a childhood summer. We talked for hours about whatever was on my mind. And sometimes we sat silently, merely enjoying each other's company. She taught me a lot about how the world works—how to sew on a button or the magic of putting ketchup on my scrambled eggs. And on one of these carefree summer days, I asked her to teach me to dance.

Nana bounced her wiry frame over to me and asked me to stand in the middle of the kitchen floor. "I'll show you the box step. Put your hand on my waist here." She grabbed my hand and placed it on her right hip and clasped my other hand in hers, lifting it near her head.

We began to dance. I placed my left foot to my left, then in front of me, then the right, then back to where I started. I slid my finger across the back of her hand, noticing prominent wrinkles firmly embedded in the leathery exterior. Nana hummed a made-up tune as our movements became swifter, keeping time by repeating the same four words: *One two three four.*

And so we danced, the minutes slipping away like hours, enjoying each other's company, pushing toward the same goal, delighting in the joy of our rhythms.

One two three four.

The mentoring relationship works much the same as dancing. Two people draw together, invited into each other's space. One leads the other, going through the motions in an effort to dance. Awkward at first, each one gives and takes in order to create the rhythm, each person taking a turn at being the leader, and then being led. Slowly, as the partners practice together and commit to the dance, their movements become one, and they dance in time to the beat of the music that is their spiritual journey.

My nana played an important part in my spiritual journey. The majority of my most relished childhood memories include her. In addition to teaching me about life, she also had an incredible hand in my spiritual formation. Every week, she took me to church, where I was introduced to God. Although my theology has changed quite a bit over the years, she instilled in me the value of consistent church attendance and the importance of being part of a church community. As a pastor's wife and church planter, this love for the church has fueled me and spurred me on "toward love and good deeds" (Heb. 10:24). If it were not for my relationship with my nana, I might not be the same person I am today.

The father in the parable is much the same as my nana in my life. She gave me everything. The minute I walked into her house, she put down what she was doing to go to church, play a game, or simply chat about the week's events. Since I wasn't close to my mother, my nana was my best friend growing up. When she died, I was devastated. It was like a part of me had died, too. Reflecting on that time together, that was God's gift to me. He gave me someone special to share her skills, wisdom, and life with me. I never for a moment thought I couldn't talk to her about something. She gave me everything she had, and she was happy to do so. Because of her willingness to invest in me mentally and emotionally, she also planted spiritual seeds in my soul as well. I wouldn't have the love for God that I have today if it were not for her. I was proud to call her my nana, and I attribute much of who I am today to her.

But it wasn't all roses. As all young girls do, one Saturday morning I spoke harsh words to my nana after she asked me to do something. "You can't tell me what to do!" I shouted, running out of her house and running back to mine. I knew I had to go back and apologize, but my pride wouldn't allow it at first. After I cooled off, I walked back to Nana's house. I was terrified to face her again. As I grew up in my house, adults never apologized. No matter what I did, I got in trouble whether it was my fault or not. Since I equated repentance with punishment, I didn't know what was ahead.

Would she ever forgive me?

Would she invite me to come over to her house?

Would she still want to be my nana?

I walked into the house and found my nana standing in her living room. When she laid eyes on me, she stretched out her arms, inviting me into an embrace. I melted into a puddle of tears. "I'm so sorry," I mumbled, burying my head in the oversized pink sweater she always wore. "It's okay," she replied, hugging me tighter. When we were done, we sat down at the kitchen table, split a bologna and cheese sandwich, and resumed our chat as usual. Not only did Nana teach me about forgiveness that day, but she also taught me about Jesus. I learned that Jesus can welcome me with open arms, no matter what I've done, and that he yearns to wrap his arms around me when I melt into a puddle of tears. I learned I could enter into God's presence no matter what I've said or done and be welcomed because my sins were already paid for a long time ago. Lastly, I learned that the banquet table is always open to me because I am his child (even if the banquet table only offers bologna and cheese).

The eldest had a mentor, too. His father gave everything to his son. He taught him how to care for the farm, gave him his inheritance before he even asked, and offered to share his place with him as host of the party rather than attender. He gave him everything, so what does the father get in return? If only the eldest saw his service as a generous payback to his father for all that the father had done for him all those years, it would make his tantrum at the end of the story a bit less childish and selfish.

The father was a mentor to both sons in a way. But the rhythm got messed up. The eldest takes care of the property, the youngest does his fair share, they both help the father as he ages, and both wait until the father dies to receive what is rightfully theirs because, after all, they wouldn't want to heap shame or disrespect on the man who had given them everything in the first place. But the prodigal didn't follow orders. He colored outside the lines, bucking cultural mores and in essence telling his father "I hate you!" when he asks for his inheritance early. Maybe that's why the eldest gets so mad at the father. If only he would stand up for decency and put the prodigal in his place. Maybe then the prodigal wouldn't have taken off, disgraced the family name, or made a fool out of his dad. But he doesn't. He doesn't do anything. He lets him get away with everything. The eldest has to stand up for what he thinks is right, an effort to right the wrongs the prodigal has committed that the father allows without caring at all about his other son. The eldest forgot that in the dance that is relationship, not everything goes as planned.

Sometimes the leader doesn't lead, causing the other dancer to get tripped up and lose his rhythm. It takes time for them to find that rhythm once again. Other times the follower wants to take over leading and takes control, leaving the leader confused as to what his role is in the whole beautiful dance. Because the roles are reversed, it makes it difficult for the leader to follow, and the follower, new to the leadership role, fumbles around aimlessly. In the story, the eldest just wants the dad to lead, to do what is right, to follow the rules society has set forth. So he steps foot in that role, telling his dad it is time to do what is right, hoping he'll do the right thing. He throws his hissy fit that rivals a two-year-old's refusal to take a nap. Did he expect his father to disown him, to do to the eldest what he should have done to the prodigal?

No, the father sends him a different message. It begins with two words:

My son.

Two beautiful words our heavenly Father says to us when we come crawling back to him after throwing our temper tantrums. The two words that accompany his outstretched arms to us just like my nana did to me after I threw my temper tantrum. Unexpected words coming from a father who did unexpected things. This is a moment eerily similar to the beginning of the story, although easy to miss if you are not looking. Why doesn't the father holler back at the son? After all, isn't the eldest doing the same thing at the end of the story that the prodigal did in the beginning? Aren't the eldest son's harsh words on par with the prodigal's taking the money and running off to waste all the money the father had earned for years of back-breaking work?

But he treats the eldest the same way he treats the prodigal: with grace. This is a pivotal moment for the eldest. How could he possibly respond after he acts that way to his father and the father still treats him with unconditional love and honor?

But it doesn't stop there. The father then says, "You are always with me, and everything I have is yours." Does it get any better than that? What could the father possibly have offered that could have topped the reminder that he has access to anything and everything he ever wanted?

Dishonoring God has been happening since the beginning of time. The beginning of Genesis with his first two children tells a similar story.

Genesis 2:20–25 says,

> But for Adam no suitable helper was found. So the LORD God caused the man to fall into a deep sleep; and while he was sleeping, he took one of the man's ribs and then closed up the place with flesh. Then the LORD God made a woman from the rib he had taken out of the man, and he brought her to the man. The man said, "This is now bone of my bones and flesh of my flesh; she shall be called 'woman,' for she was taken out of man." That is why a man leaves his father and mother and is united to his wife, and they become one flesh. Adam and his wife were both naked, and they felt no shame.

Before the fall, Adam and Eve accepted themselves for who they were. They were content with their love for each other as well as God's love for them. Verse 25 is particularly significant, because being naked meant they were fully exposed before God and each other, and they were okay with it! There were no secrets, no reason to hide anything from the other. They knew each other fully, and nothing stood in the way of having the fullness of fellowship and intimacy God desired for them.

In fact, they were placed in the garden for two reasons:

- **Fellowship with God:** God wanted to live in paradise forever with his children. But when they ate the fruit, they demonstrated that their independence was more important to them than dependence on him.
- **Fellowship with each other:** God intends for us to accept each other as we truly are. We shouldn't need affirmation from each other, because God's approval is sufficient. We were meant to coexist in a way that gives life to our souls.

Once Satan had tricked Eve into believing there was more to life wrapped up in the sweet, savory taste of that fruit, they struggled with seeing God as a loving father who has given them everything they could need or want, too. Before the fall, they enjoyed the fullness of fellowship with God, completely exposed to God in everything, including their physical, mental, and spiritual lives. After the fall, the feeling of shame crept in, and soon it was no longer acceptable in their eyes to be fully exposed. They made coverings for themselves, and soon not only were their physical parts covered, but their spiritual, emotional, and mental parts were also marred by sin.

> When the woman saw that the fruit of the tree was good for food and pleasing to the eye, and also desirable for gaining wisdom, she took some and ate it. She also gave some to her husband, who was with her, and he ate it. Then the eyes of both of them were opened, and they realized they were naked; so they sewed fig leaves together and made coverings for themselves. Then the man and his wife heard the sound of the LORD God as he was walking in the garden in the cool of the day, and they hid from the LORD God among the trees of the garden. But the LORD God called to the man, "Where are you?" (Gen. 3:6–9)

When we sin, it is our tendency to want to hide, pretending that God is not omniscient and that he cannot see us for who we are or what we have done. But God sees everything. There are no places where we can hide from God. Like Adam and Eve, we can deceive ourselves into thinking that we can give God an excuse for our behavior and that we can deceive him into believing our lie. But

God is truth. It is in his nature. He knew what we would do even before we did it. All he wants from us, just as he wanted from his first children, is for us to take responsibility for our sin and bring every part of ourselves to God to regain the fullness of intimacy he intended for us.

Do you see how repentance is the key, both in Genesis and the prodigal son parable? God wanted to remove the sin from Adam and Eve, just as he wanted to extend grace to the eldest. God is not a God of condemnation. However, he does judge us, because he is a God of justice and of grace. When he asks Adam and Eve, "Where are you?" it is not because he doesn't know where they are. On the contrary, he offers them an opportunity to take responsibility, to repent, to ask for forgiveness from an almighty God who was waiting to welcome them back into his fellowship, if they'd have him. But they took the easy road, blaming each other. The world has been doing it ever since. The eldest blamed the father for the prodigal's sins just like Adam and Eve blamed each other. Now our sin comes with a heavy weight of shame attached to it, a feeling God never wanted us to have.

The father wanted that communion with his son, too. "My son" was the indication that the eldest had gotten it wrong. He was always welcome in the family of God, if only he would come in and have a seat at the table. The "everything I have is yours" statement was the father's reward that was already waiting for him for being faithful and true for all those years. The eldest was looking for some sort of approval from his father, but the father's words tell him he had it all along. The father celebrates us simply because we are his children. The eldest is the father's son, whom he loves, a son he loves and cherishes, just as he loves the Pharisees, too. Isn't that enough reason to celebrate?

DISCUSSION QUESTIONS

1 Have you ever felt that God has not adequately rewarded you for your faithfulness to him?

2 In this chapter, I told a story about my nana forgiving me after we had had a fight. Her gesture of forgiveness spoke volumes to me and showed me what God's love is truly like. Have you ever had a situation where you learned about forgiveness from someone? What did you learn?

3 Every relationship is like a dance in which both partners give and take so they can keep their rhythm. Think of a situation when you lost your rhythm with that person. What happened that made you lose your rhythm? What did you do to regain it?

Chapter Twelve

Breaking Free from the Religious Spirit

Now that we have fully understood who the eldest is and how the religious spirit can take hold of our lives before we even know it, we can work toward breaking free of the bondage it can have on us.

BUILDING UP AND NOT TEARING DOWN

Before the fall, Adam and Eve lived in community with each other. They didn't need anyone else's approval because God accepted them fully for who they were.

Once they ate the fruit, however, their perspective changed. No longer was God's knowledge enough. They looked to others for their approval; they depended on others to tell them they were good enough. One word shows exactly when their self-esteem changed: *realized*. "Then the eyes of both of them were opened, and they realized they were naked" (Gen. 3:7).

God pursued them in the garden and gave them a chance for redemption by asking, "Where are you?" Adam replied, "I heard you in the garden, and I was afraid because I was naked, so I hid." Our fears about being accepted when we are exposed started with Adam's fear about being naked. Being naked physically before the fall meant living fully in freedom from sin and insecurity. Being naked after the fall meant God could see everything, even the deepest parts of Adam.

Knowing he had disobeyed God and being aware of God's sudden disapproval was more than Adam could handle. He hid both his body and his soul from God, perhaps hoping God wouldn't notice. God offered Adam the chance to return to the garden and live with him in paradise, but instead of taking the opportunity, Adam decided to blame God: "The woman you put with me . . ." He didn't take responsibility and confess his sin before God; instead, he sewed fig leaves together not only to cover his body, but also his soul. No longer could God live with his children in peace and perfect harmony. The unconfessed sin had been sown into Adam's heart, separating him from full communion with his heavenly Father.

But there's hope.

God offered the olive branch of hope and communion with his children once again with the death of his Son, Jesus. Jesus's death provided us the opportunity to fully bare our hearts and souls before God, so we can receive the healing and reconciliation we need to live in the security of God's love for us.

The eldest also tries to tear down his father and brother. But there is hope as well. As we have discussed, an incessant need to tear others down is a sign of a religious spirit that has crept into the soul. For one week, seek to say nothing negative about anyone, not on Facebook, not to others, and not to yourself. See how much your attitude changes.

LIVE LOVED

Until I knew the Lord, I felt less than. Wearing glasses in middle school, I was automatically dubbed a nerd. My glasses paired with doing well in school equaled being out of the inner circle of the popular crowds. Because I didn't look like what society believed was good looking, I often felt left out of activities, parties, and inner circles. From an early age, I equated appearance with worth. Because of this, my *good enough* quickly became *less than.*

Even the first woman, Eve, struggled with less than. Once Satan put doubt in her mind that there was more out there, her good enough world of paradise quickly became less than.

We all struggle with wanting more. First Samuel 16:7 says: "But the LORD said to Samuel, 'Don't judge by his appearance or height, for I have rejected him. The LORD doesn't see things the way you see them. People judge by outward appearance, but the LORD looks at the heart'" (NLT).

According to this passage, every one of his family thought David was less than. Because he was the youngest of his family, everyone overlooked his potential to be king. Because he didn't look like the ideal candidate, everyone dismissed him. Yet, God saw his heart. He knew the kindness and zeal to obey God that was deep within David. Because of these qualities, God knew he had what it took to fulfill his royal responsibilities.

David was not chosen because he did everything right. God loved him because of who he was. God loves you for who you are, too. Despite what you look like, despite your past, despite how smart you think you are.

Society bases everything on looks. From the newest magazine showcasing the hottest airbrushed model to being judged based on what car you drive, outward appearance is what most people use to determine if someone has worth and value.

But that's not what God uses. God knows your heart. He knows everything you have ever done, ever said, ever thought. He knew you before you were born. He knows your capabilities, even if you feel overlooked by the world. A constant feeling of being overlooked can skew your view of who God is, hindering you from knowing God fully.

God sees everything. He knows you and loves you. When you understand that God judges your worth based on who you are rather than what you do or what you look like, you will begin to understand and accept God's love for you.

Jennifer Dukes Lee, author of *The Happiness Dare,* says,

> I had lost the fullness of my happiness and I didn't know where to find it. What I'm going to tell you next might sound a little crazy, but it's the truth: During those times of unhappiness, my great comfort came in believing that God didn't care about happiness anyway. My great comfort came in believing God cared more about my holiness. So I figured, *If I can't be happy, I'm still good with God.* My holiness, then, became an excuse to stop seeking happiness.
>
> This is a tragic error of Christians everywhere. Welcome to the atrophy of the human soul. But this is where some of us are right now. We are highly suspicious of happiness. We really *do* want to be happy—secretly of course—but we'll tell everyone else it's joy we want. Because isn't joy the holier aim? Isn't happiness against the rules?[1]

Being Your Authentic Self

When I was in the fourth grade, I began to have headaches every day after I came home from school. When I was in school, I had trouble seeing the blackboard. For months I suffered with this, until my mother took me to the eye doctor. After my screening, the optometrist declared that I needed glasses. Initially excited, I chose a pair of lavender-colored glasses, my favorite color. I couldn't wait until I got to school to show off my new specs.

That was, until I got my first taste of ridicule. People talking behind my back, calling me names, was devastating. Being told I was a nerd because of my glasses made me wear contact lenses every day after I received them when I was sixteen, never letting anyone see me with my glasses. Recently, however, I have noticed that a nagging dry eye paired with flimsy contact lenses has forced me to wear my glasses more often, even out in public. I thought my first run-in with someone I knew at the grocery store would cause me great embarrassment, making me want to duck into the produce aisle and avoid the acquaintance until they left the store. But I felt eerily confident and talked to the person with ease. When they left, I wasn't embarrassed at all; in fact, it felt a bit freeing.

Being known for who you truly are without the need to cover yourself up is restoring the freedom the eldest could have had with his father. If only the eldest had stopped keeping score of what his brother had versus what he had and lived in the freedom of the generous love his father bestowed on him each and every day. That's the freedom God intended for us to have, to approach him holding nothing back, allowing him to love us just as we are.

If I had worried less about what others thought and more about what God thought, I might have been happier with who I was. But I internalized those remarks, allowing them to affect the whole of who I was. This caused me to wear contact lenses in public, makeup on my face, and trendy clothes on my body, all in an effort to cover up who I was.

When we put on a false self to others instead of being who we are, we want to cover up who we are instead of exposing ourselves to others. We believe a lie that who we are is not good enough.

False selves can deceive us too. It tricked the eldest into believing society's perceptions were more valuable than his father's approval. It deceives others into believing you are someone you are not, and it deceives you into believing your worth comes from places other than God.

Embrace your weaknesses as well as your strengths. Be proud of who you are, knowing that everyone has flaws. Don't try to be perfect, but live in the reality that perfection is a myth. This is the first step in leaving your false self behind and embracing your real self.

TAKE OFF YOUR MASK

As I hopped out of the shower to get ready for the day, I dressed in my prettiest top and pants and prepared to embark on my daily beauty regimen of putting on my makeup. I applied my foundation like a painter applying a coat of primer, careful to cover every flaw and imperfection from the naked eye. As I worked, I felt God gently whisper to my heart, "Why do you need to cover your flaws? You are beautiful in spite of your flaws." Like many women, I believed the lie that my worth is based on my physical appearance, not on my inward characteristics. In response, I took my washcloth and washed it all off. Then I went to church. You know what happened?

Nothing.

No one commented on my lack of makeup. No one criticized my seemingly unkempt appearance.

I realized that I was using my makeup not only as a physical technique to cover my imperfections, but also like a mask to pretend that I had it all together. Deep down, I thought that if people saw my flaws, they might not like me as a person. What a terrifying feeling! But even more terrifying is not being who God has made me to be. When I put my worth in Christ and not in others' perceptions of me, what people think of me becomes less important. Second Corinthians 3:18 says, "But we all, with unveiled faces, beholding as in a mirror the glory of the Lord, are being transformed into the same image from glory to glory, just as from the Lord, the Spirit" (NASB).

Perhaps you can relate. Maybe you don't wear makeup, but you use other areas of life as a mask to cover your insecurities. Maybe you use clothing tricks to cover your body's trouble zones. Perhaps you use food or drink to medicate the pain your past has caused. But God wants us as his disciples to take off the masks in our lives and let the world see who we truly are.

A. M. Allchin, author of *The World Is a Wedding*, writes, "The way that leads to perfect joy which comes from the knowledge and the love of God is one which goes by the way of extreme paradox. We find the fullness of God at the moment of man's greatest emptiness."[2] Similarly, in *Closer Walk: 365 Devotions that Nurture a Heart for God*, F. B. Meyer writes,

> The elder brother is the dark contrast which heightens the glowing picture of the repentant prodigal. When we look at sin, not in its theological aspects but in its everyday clothes, we find that it divides itself into two kinds. We find there are sins of the body and sins of the disposition; or, more narrowly, sins of the passions, including all forms of lust and selfishness, and sins of the temper.
>
> The prodigal is the instance in the New Testament of sins of passion; the elder brother of sins of temper. One scholar did a careful analysis of the ingredients that went

> into that one spiteful speech. They were jealousy, anger, pride, uncharity, cruelty, self-righteousness, sulkiness, and touchiness.[3]

How can someone live in the love and approval of his father if he struggles with so much anger, hurt, and sheer disappointment? It's obvious the eldest son didn't fully understand the sheer joy of being loved and accepted by his father simply for who he was, not what he did. It's obvious from the father's display that he doesn't conform to the norms of hiding his affection from his sons, so why didn't the eldest talk to his dad about his hurts and work through them? A year and a half ago, I started a grief journal to write down all the losses in my life to help me process them. This was useful, because so many hurts came up that I did not know were there. I can't live in the freedom of love God wants for me if I'm living with pent-up anger and resentment over others' actions. To break free, the eldest must somehow resolve his hurts before he can go into that party. Otherwise, he will go in as a host and resent his guests. That's not only impolite but also detrimental to all his relationships. It's time for the eldest to bury his hurts out in the field, accept the father's invitation, and enjoy the feast before time runs out.

Tommi Femrite writes,

> There was a time in my life when I was more interested in what people thought than what God thought. Oh, I may have said I was interested in what God thought, but my actions proved otherwise. Much to my amazement I realized that I was bound by a religious spirit. What followed was a journey to discover how this spirit not only operated in my life and moved through other people but also

> had power over me. I soon realized that the battle was over my soul—my mind, my will and my emotions. . . .
>
> Have you ever whined before the Lord and said, "I am all alone. No one cares about me. No one even knows I'm here"? The religious spirit will have you think that God has abandoned you or that he doesn't even know your name or that he may know your name but he doesn't care about you any more, since he has left you all alone to fend for yourself. But don't be deceived. This is not God's character. God does not do or say things like this.[4]

As I write this book, the country is embarking on the most historic and polarizing election in our history. Two unsavory candidates are running to secure their position as the leader of the United States, and Christians are more divided than ever. When the results were announced, half of the Christians shouted with joy. The other half scowled and posted false articles on Facebook to make themselves feel better for not voting for the winner. Throughout this election, people have shamed others into voting for their candidate, swept their candidates' deeds under the rug in the name of saving the country, and slandered the other candidate in the name of "speaking the truth in love." This election has been eye-opening to me in a few ways:

Christians blindly believe what the media tells them without checking the validity of their statements.

History is repeating itself in that everyone did what was right in their own eyes, without giving heed to wise counsel or the spiritual teachers and leaders within their churches.

Christians lack the discernment to make good decisions or rely on the wise counsel of others to help them make good decisions.

WAYS TO BREAK FREE FROM THE RELIGIOUS SPIRIT

It is obvious that the prodigal lacked that wisdom when he went traipsing off to his wild living, but what about the eldest? Didn't he lack the discernment to know that his father loved him just as much as he loved the prodigal? Did he take the father's advice to come in to the party and make amends, or did he stand outside pouting and shaming the father for making such poor family decisions? Neither the actions of the eldest nor the actions of Christians today seem to warrant our separation from the father. He still pleads with us to come in instead of standing out in the cold (which is where we deserve to be more often than not).

ERASE THE NEGATIVE SELF-TALK

We all have statements we have said to ourselves since we were small children. Some have been deeply ingrained and some are fairly new, but all of them have made an indelible mark on our hearts and minds. Perhaps a parent repeated the mantra, "You'll never amount to anything." A high school boyfriend berated you by saying, "Why don't you stop dressing so provocatively? Then maybe I will like you better." Maybe a teacher made you feel stupid as you answered a question in class incorrectly. Soon, we begin to believe the negative statements people say to us and make it a part of the self-talk that plays in our minds. Whatever statements you say to yourself, you are not alone. We all have had naysayers try to knock us down instead of building us up. No matter what you repeat to yourself on a regular basis, it can be erased. God's Word is full of the truth of who you are in God's eyes. Every time you repeat statements that are against the Word of God, the devil has a reason to stake a claim in your life.

But there's hope. Study the Word and hide it in your heart. It may sound cliché, but when Jesus was tempted in the desert, his only line of defense was the Word of God he had known since he was a boy. That study of the Law did not return void, and it won't in your life either. Commit to memorizing one Scripture a week. Soon you will have fifty-two scriptures that speak to the promises of who you are in God's eyes.

As Christians, we all have dealt with negative self-talk. It is not enough for us to simply not dwell on it; we must replace it with the truth of Scripture. We owe it to ourselves. When Jesus was in a low time, he only had Scripture to rely on when Satan tempted him after his forty days of fasting. If he can defeat Satan using the truth of God's Word, so can we. But we have to hide the Word in our hearts so it can emerge when we are tempted to let our fears reign supreme.

For example:

> Your head says, "I can't do this on my own."
> God's Word says, "When I am weak, then I am strong" (2 Cor. 12:10).

> Your head says, "I am not good enough."
> God's Word says, "We are children of God" (1 John 3:1–2).

> Your head says, "I'm not pretty enough."
> God's Word says, "Charm is deceptive, and beauty is fleeting; but a woman who fears the LORD is to be praised" (Prov. 31:30).

Negative people, circumstances, and situations can sometimes leave indelible marks on our souls. But God doesn't want us to stay that way. Knowing and meditating on Scripture can erase even the most devastating comment. If we can erase our negative self-talk, we can replace those lies with the truth of who we are in Christ.

TAKE EVERY THOUGHT CAPTIVE

> *For the weapons of our warfare are not of the flesh, but divinely powerful for the destruction of fortresses. We are destroying speculations and every lofty thing raised up against the knowledge of God, and we are taking every thought captive to the obedience of Christ. (2 Cor. 10:4–5 NASB)*

I have heard that verse many times, but what does it really mean to take every thought captive?

The Bible has a lot to say about the ways in which we can control our thoughts. Our fears begin in our mind. However, if we do not discern whether or not those thoughts are contributing to our well-being or leading us down the path to sin, sin can quickly find a home within our hearts. The apostle Paul had some experience with making thoughts obedient to Christ: "Finally, brothers and sisters, whatever is true, whatever is noble, whatever is right, whatever is pure, whatever is lovely, whatever is admirable—if anything is excellent or praiseworthy—think about such things" (Phil. 4:8).

Here are some questions to ask yourself if you want to practice taking your thoughts captive following the pattern outlined in Philippians:

Is it true?

Is it noble?

Is it right?

Is it pure?

Is it lovely?

Is it admirable?

If your tendency is to keep the thought a secret rather than tell someone, it is from Satan, not from God. If it doesn't line up with the basic concepts you know from Scripture, such thoughts are not something you want to dwell on for long.

The world wants you to dwell on lies instead of the truth. Scripture gives us a clear way to combat this problem: take every thought captive. Pastor Steven Furtick says you should interrogate every thought like cops do with criminals. We should question a thought and know its very origin before we decide if we should believe it.

That's what God wants to do with our lives. He doesn't want us to shove our fears down through control, but to question them. If the thoughts contributing to the fear are from God, fear can prevent us from making a mistake or going down a wrong path. If the thoughts are from the enemy, they need to be discarded. Using the gift of discernment God gave us through his Word can be the first key to transitioning from a life of cowardice to a life of boldness.

CONNECT THROUGH COMMUNITY

One day, as I was praying about the different avenues of growing in my spiritual life, I realized I had been missing a spiritual mentor, someone with whom I could connect on a regular basis for accountability, prayer, and advice. After much prayer and consideration, I selected a woman who I connected with at a promotional event for our books. Since we are both writers, this was a great match from the start. We call each other each week and share what we learn from a book about writing we have been reading. We also discuss areas in which we want to grow, and we end our discussion with prayer requests. Although it is only fifteen minutes a week, I can't imagine going a week without talking with her. She has become a confidante, and I am proud to call her my friend.

In the parable of the prodigal, it is interesting that the eldest was out in the field alone. Isolation is where Satan can play tricks on us. The anger the eldest was feeling over the father's willingness to give both sons their inheritance was already present. But it is in isolation where his heart can grow callous against his brother. What if the father had been in the field, working alongside him? What if he had carried on his mentoring relationship out in the field and spoken to the son as they cared for the property together? Would anger still have had room to remain? Community is essential, not only in the eldest's life, but also in the life of a believer. Community helps us find wise counsel from others who can pray with us and encourage us; we hear wise instruction and we enjoy the gift of fellowship. If only the eldest had had a community of support around him, it would have helped him not care so much about what society thought and more about what God thought.

In life, we are also to embark on our spiritual journeys together rather than apart. But so often, Satan deceives us into thinking that we can do the Christian life on our own. We substitute a sermon on TV for church services, individual Bible studies for small groups, and individual prayer time for accountability with others. While all these things are good for our souls, we are also meant to do things in community. Even in the Gospels, Jesus always sends out the twelve apostles in pairs to heal the sick, drive out demons, and preach the good news. Even Noah and the animals entered the ark two by two!

Having a community of brothers and sisters in Christ that you can go to for support, encouragement, and challenge is vital in helping you grow in your walk with God and gain a better understanding of who he is. The most important thing you can do to help develop your self-concept is to get connected with a church on a regular basis. As you attend regularly and serve selflessly, you will bond with other people like you who have the same goal of walking closely with God, and you'll break free from that religious spirit that diminishes God to a set of strictly followed rules.

WALK IN THE LIGHT

> *The life appeared; we have seen it and testify to it, and we proclaim to you the eternal life, which was with the Father and has appeared to us. We proclaim to you what we have seen and heard, so that you also may have fellowship with us. And our fellowship is with the Father and with his Son, Jesus Christ. We write this to make our joy complete. This is the message we have heard from him and declare to you: God is light; in him there is no darkness at all. If we claim to have fellowship with him and yet walk in the darkness, we lie and do not live out the truth. But if we walk in the light, as he is in the light, we have fellowship with one another, and the blood of Jesus, his Son, purifies us from all sin. (1 John 1:2–7)*

In the postmodern world in which we live, truth is becoming more and more distorted each day. The morally relativistic world in which we live dictates that we should each speak "our truth," implying that your truth may not be the same as my truth, and that what works for you may not necessarily work for me. Yet, the Bible is the anchor that holds all of the truths together. In an article regarding Christianity and truth, author Dick Tripp wrote:

> A [1992] Barna Research Group survey on what Americans believe asked the question, "Is there absolute Truth?" Sixty-six percent of adults responded that they believe that "there is no such thing as absolute truth; different people can define truth in conflicting ways and still be correct." Seventy-two percent of those aged 18 to 25 expressed this belief. In a recent series of more than twenty interviews

> conducted at random at a large university, people were asked if there was such a thing as absolute truth—truth that is true across all times and cultures for all people. All but one respondent answered along these lines:
>
> "Truth is whatever you believe."
>
> "There is no absolute truth."
>
> "If there *were* such a thing as absolute truth, how could we know what it is?"
>
> "People who believe in absolute truth are dangerous."
>
> The lone exception was an evangelical Christian, who said absolute truth was in Jesus Christ.[5]

The only way we can navigate through this ever-confusing world of truths and fallacies is if we walk hand in hand with someone who is anchored in the truth and is not easily swayed by the world's beliefs.

Through living in community with others in deep fellowship, we too can walk in the light as Jesus did. John, James, and Peter got a taste of this physical light as they witnessed Jesus's transfiguration on the mountain:

> Six days later Jesus took Peter and the two brothers, James and John, and led them up a high mountain to be alone. As the men watched, Jesus' appearance was transformed so that his face shone like the sun, and his clothes became as white as light. Suddenly, Moses and Elijah appeared and began talking with Jesus.
>
> Peter exclaimed, "Lord, it's wonderful for us to be here! If you want, I'll make three shelters as memorials—one for you, one for Moses, and one for Elijah."
>
> But even as he spoke, a bright cloud overshadowed them, and a voice from the cloud said, "This is my dearly

> loved Son, who brings me great joy. Listen to him." The disciples were terrified and fell face down on the ground.
>
> Then Jesus came over and touched them. "Get up," he said. "Don't be afraid." And when they looked up, Moses and Elijah were gone, and they saw only Jesus. (Matt. 17:1–8 NLT)

Jesus established a sense of trust and honesty with these three men, enough to trust them with seeing him in his most divine state. Similarly, John, James, and Peter, although flawed, must have demonstrated a great sense of maturity, enough for Jesus to invest in them on a personal level. These are the type of people you as a leader need to find. Who has demonstrated enough maturity that you should devote your time, energy, and resources to develop them into a leader and spokesperson for the gospel? Because of this event, John, James, and Peter understood what it meant to truly walk in the light, both literally and figuratively. Not only did they need to follow the teachings of Jesus, but they also had to invest in each other. This helped build their trust in each other, enough to walk together as they went from town to town spreading the good news, healing people, and driving out demons.

The fellowship that satiates our parched soul only comes from honest, authentic fellowship with others. However, not everyone is suited to enjoy that kind of fellowship. A couple of years ago, my husband and I began to share our lives with a couple from our church. He began to share some of his struggles in passing during the workday, and I began to share similar struggles during times of fun and recreation. We believed we could trust the people we shared with because, on the outside, they demonstrated what we believed was spiritual maturity. However, when the church took a turn this couple didn't like, they twisted what was said and used it to try to turn the church against us. When we finally confronted them, we were able to refute all of the claims made and proved them to be lies. It was a devastating blow to us, not only because we thought they were friends, but also because we had believed they were growing spiritually, when in reality they were spiritually stuck. This caused us to exercise great caution in the future when faced with the decision of whom we could trust to partner with to truly walk in the light.

BE THANKFUL

I have known how to pray since I was a child. With a quick "Dear Lord," I'd summon God like using a gumball machine, inserting my coin and waiting for the magic treat to land in my hand. I'd ask for whatever I wanted, and I expected God to deliver my every whim and desire like a genie in a bottle. But when I began an intimate relationship with Jesus at the age of eighteen, I didn't get everything I wanted. It was downright frustrating. I mean, isn't that the purpose of communing with God?

As in any relationship, both parties involved must give to the other in order to make it successful. Although there are times when one must take and the other give, balance must be achieved or else the relationship becomes one-sided. In my relationship with God, I can give God nothing, as he has all he needs. The one thing I can give him is my gratitude and thanks for all he does, even if it doesn't arrive in the way or in the time I think it should. Scripture is clear: "Do not be anxious about anything, but in every situation, by prayer and petition, with thanksgiving, present your requests to God" (Phil. 4:6).

One of the biggest stumbling blocks to understanding our freedom in Christ is contentment. When we place our value in what we have or what we do rather than being grateful for what

God has given us, we tend to ignore what is truly important. If we're not grateful for how God made us, our view of our physical beauty is distorted, as well as our attitude about our emotional and spiritual beauty.

New York Times best-selling author Ann Voskamp shares her perspective on the connection between the fall of man and ingratitude:

> From all of our beginnings, we keep reliving the Garden story. Satan, he wanted more. More power, more glory. Ultimately, in his essence, Satan is an ingrate. And he sinks his venom into the heart of Eden. Satan's sin becomes the first sin of all humanity: *the sin of ingratitude.* Adam and Eve are simply, painfully, ungrateful for what God gave. Isn't that the catalyst of all my sins? Our fall was, has always been, and always will be, that we aren't satisfied in God and what He gives. We hunger for something more, something other.[6]

There's nothing wrong with wanting to improve ourselves physically, mentally, or spiritually. But when we view ourselves as unworthy of love or value simply because of our looks, we are focusing on the wrong things. Jesus never meant for us to live in bondage to a poor self-image. Regardless of the things you have done or the things that have been done to you, God wants you to live in the freedom that you are loved, accepted, and approved exactly as you are.

God does not love us any less because someone else is skinnier, prettier, or more popular than we are. The sooner we understand that, the sooner we can accept ourselves for who we are, and the temptation to compare ourselves to others will decrease. Jesus wants us to be content with his will for our lives. Constantly looking over our shoulders, concerned with what someone else has, is an endless pursuit.

Anger flees in the face of thanksgiving. When I am focused on being thankful, I don't have time to be angry or hurt. When I am thankful, I am content with whatever God gives, whenever he decides to give it.

RELEASE THE FEAR

The religious spirit is driven by fear, insecurity, and anxiety. The Holy Spirit we receive is different. Romans 8:14–17 says,

> For those who are led by the Spirit of God are the children of God. The Spirit you received does not make you slaves, so that you live in fear again; rather, the Spirit you received brought about your adoption to sonship. And by him we cry, "Abba, Father." The Spirit himself testifies with our spirit that we are God's children. Now if we are children, then we are heirs—heirs of God and co-heirs with Christ, if indeed we share in his sufferings in order that we may also share in his glory.

Receive the Father's grace and experience it. Receive the gift of the Holy Spirit, that by his power we can call God "Abba" or "Daddy."

RELEASE THE RELIGION

We are coheirs with Christ. That means we need to release all the false ways of trying to earn our identity or prove who we are. Insecurity is almost always behind the religious spirit. This manifests as trying to find your significance and value in what you can or can't do, what you do or don't have, or what others say about you. So your activity is all about trying to build your life on that false sense of being. If you want to find freedom and revival, you need to release those patterns in your life. Your significance and value aren't found in what you do or by your appearing to have everything together. Your father loves you. Release the need to earn your identity or to look like you have it all together. Release those comparisons. Release self-effort.

RESPOND TO GOD'S GRACE

The father says, "But we had to celebrate and be glad, because this brother of yours was dead and is alive again; he was lost and is found." Respond in worship. Respond in celebration of what God is doing. When we worship (or in the eldest's case, celebrate), it takes the focus off us and places the focus on God. Revival is all about God and what he does. It's his work. Don't try to earn it. Receive his grace and respond through celebration.

RECALIBRATE YOUR LIFE

Unfortunately, we don't know how the older brother responded to the father in Jesus's story. But his point was for us to respond. We need to recalibrate our idea of what it means to grow. We need to come up with a new scorecard. The Pharisees' scorecard had to do with all the outward stuff. It had to do with getting the behavior right. Jesus told them they were like whitewashed tombs: they looked really pretty on the outside but were dead on the inside. The new scorecard for maturity needs to come from Christ. Proverbs 4:23 says, "Above all else, guard your heart, for everything you do flows from it." Pursue a love relationship with God with your entire being: heart, soul, mind, and strength.

If you get the heart right, everything else will fall in line.

DISCUSSION QUESTIONS

1 Did you find any of the suggestions listed in this chapter helpful in breaking free of the religious spirit in your life?

2 Do you find it difficult to live an authentic life in front of others? Why or why not?

3 What actions could you take as a result of this chapter to ensure that you break free from the hold the religious spirit has on your life?

NOTES

[1]Jenifer Dukes Lee, *The Happiness Dare* (Grand Rapids: Waterbrook, 2016), 8.

[2]A. M. Allchin, *The World Is a Wedding: Explorations in Christian Spirituality* (Oxford: Oxford University Press, 1979), 5.

[3]Bruce H. Wilkinson, ed., *Closer Walk: 365 Daily Devotions That Nurture a Heart for God* (Grand Rapids: Zondervan, 1992), 100.

[4]Tommi Femrite, "Protecting Your Soul from the Spirit of Religion," in *Freedom from the Religious Spirit*, 89, 92.

[5]Dick Tripp, "What Is Truth and Does It Matter?" Grace Communion International, https://www.gci.org/series/truth1, based on an article in *Christianity Today*, October 26, 1992, 30.

[6]Ann Voskamp, *One Thousand Gifts* (Grand Rapids: Zondervan, 2010), 14.

Chapter Thirteen

Final Reflections on the Eldest Brother

As we conclude our journey together of diving deep into the parable of the prodigal son, I hope you have come away with a few nuggets of truth, some eye-opening revelations, and most of all, a new understanding that the people written about in the Bible are more like us than we think. When I first became a Christian, I didn't see myself in any of the people I read about between the pages of that sacred book.

They're just stories, I thought.

But when I stopped reading it to simply check it off my to-do list and instead pored over commentaries and allowed the Holy Spirit to guide me in gaining wisdom, I realized I was just like Martha, who threw her dishtowel in disgust from the food she carefully prepared to host the Savior of the world. I nodded my head in agreement as Peter turned to the man who was merciful enough to give him a second chance and said, "What about him?" I wept with Jeremiah as he shouted God's Word from the rooftops, only to have it fall on deaf ears. The more I humbled myself, the more I understood that God used those sinners during that period of history, and now he is using this sinner today.

Since there is nothing new under the sun, as Ecclesiastes proclaims, every person God chooses to use to further his kingdom has strengths and weaknesses just like me, and the eldest brother is no different. Upon first glance at the parable, he is forgettable, easily missed, yet he carries so much weight within the story and he has lessons for all of us. From being a representation of Jesus as our older brother to contemplating an invitation from the father to host both sinner and saint, we can all find a little bit of ourselves in the eldest brother, can't we?

We've all grumbled and complained at our father's seeming injustice. We've all felt the slow and steady release as our once prideful egos deflate a bit further at watching some God-forsaken heathen emerge from far away, worming his way into the father's heart and taking what's rightfully ours. What an ungrateful brother the prodigal is. His selfishness is enough to make us sever ties with him, and rightfully so. He squandered his time with his brother, substituting a rich relationship filled with true fellowship for the opportunity to live it up with his friends. Who would do that?

Me, and so would you.

We squander our opportunity for fellowship and connection with others all the time. We squander our time by worshiping the idols we have erected in place of a real relationship with Christ. We pretend we have fellowship when we attend all the obligatory church programs and services, hoping to find favor not with God but with the brothers and sisters we claim to love. We compare and compete, satiating our thirst for fortune and fame through our service and pseudo-communities we create. We pretend we don't need anything—after all, we have cared for the property God has entrusted to us for so many years; we can handle all of it ourselves. When deep down, even though our lives look as though we have it all together, the one thing we want more than any possession or party is the deep affection and approval of the father.

QUEEN OF THE PITY PARTY

Perhaps the words of Jesus to the Pharisees about how to have a party are the ones the eldest needed to hear the most:

> When he noticed how the guests picked the places of honor at the table, he told them this parable:
>
> "When someone invites you to a wedding feast, do not take the place of honor, for a person more distinguished than you may have been invited. If so, the host who invited both of you will come and say to you, 'Give this person your seat.' Then, humiliated, you will have to take the least important place. But when you are invited, take the lowest place, so that when your host comes, he will say to you, 'Friend, move up to a better place.' Then you will be honored in the presence of all the other guests. For all those who exalt themselves will be humbled, and those who humble themselves will be exalted."
>
> Then Jesus said to his host, "When you give a luncheon or dinner, do not invite your friends, your brothers or sisters, your relatives, or your rich neighbors; if you do, they may invite you back and so you will be repaid. But when you give a banquet, invite the poor, the crippled, the lame, the blind, and you will be blessed. Although

> they cannot repay you, you will be repaid at the resurrection of the righteous." (Luke 14:7–14)

The host wanted to move him to a higher place, the place he deserved for all his years of hard work. But that simply wasn't good enough. Just like when I wrestled with God as to why I had to constantly be second in the spelling bee, lose perfect attendance, and not be salutatorian, God was preparing me for a banquet feast of his own. But first, he needed to do the work of humbling me, in order to exalt me later. Being able to write this book and be a mouthpiece of the gospel through the stringing together of words is a privilege I do not take lightly. As I type furiously on my keyboard, I am constantly reminded of the people who also were second in the eyes of the world—David, Leah, Joseph, just to name a few. God had to humble them so they could be exalted later. Through them he did great things that not only accomplished his work but also changed the world. Without celebrating being second, the opportunity to celebrate being first is not as sweet. Without laboring in the field, the opportunity to be an honored host is not as cherished. Without cultivating the very fare dined on in that feast, how could enjoying the fruits of that labor be so sweet?

Without the hard work, tears, and perseverance through the tough times in my life, I would not be the person I am today. I can choose to look down at my lot in life, kick the sand, and whine about how things aren't going my way. If I'm honest, I spent a lot of my life doing that. As I indicated in an earlier chapter, the lie that I was unseen and forgotten by the world because I was not the favorite in my family permeated every area of my life. I distinctly remember when I was young, my mother gave my sister a candy bar. As she did so, she said, "And I have to give one to Michelle so everything is fair." On the surface, that would sound like a loving statement, but the eye roll she added made me feel like she was only doing it out of pity and not out of love. That feeling of only being added as an afterthought was planted deep in the back of my mind, compounded by the instances in school where I didn't receive the things I worked so hard for, and it gave me every opportunity to throw myself a party that rivaled that of the prodigal son, complete with griping, gossiping, and anger.

Because of that event, I was constantly griping about all the things I never received. This did nothing to help me grow closer to God. In fact, it just pulled me away, because it distorted what I thought about myself and how I viewed others as being favored or loved by God more than me. I was the one and only guest at my party. By my standard, I would have been the poor mentioned in Jesus's words to the Pharisees regarding inviting the poor to your feast, because I was poor indeed—poor in spirit.

But like there was hope for the eldest, there is hope for us too.

There's still a party to be had. The parable ends with the decision placed on the eldest as to whether or not he will accept. What if he never goes into the party, never smells the fatted calf that has been cooked to perfection, never runs his fingers across the fine china set out for the guest of honor? He never hears the cheers of the other guests at the party, slapping the prodigal on the back as a sign of acceptance. He never tastes the sweet wine or raises his glass in acknowledgment of the one who turned his back on his wild life and one who worked to be the glue to keep the father and all his possessions in order.

The eldest has a choice, and so do we. Will you keep living a life of ingratitude, anger, and pain, or will you swallow your pride, step into the house, and toast your guests?

Take the father's hand and enjoy. The guests are waiting for you.

Chapter Fourteen

Stories from the Modern-Day Pharisee

As I finished this book, I reveled in how much I had learned about myself and others. As I strive to discard my Pharisaic lifestyle, I thought I could learn (and take solace) in the fact that many Christians have acted more like a Pharisee than I realize. So I asked some of my friends if they would share their stories of bring a Pharisee. Here is what one person shared:

> I love to memorize Scripture. So far I've memorized the book of Philippians, the book of Ruth, the first three chapters of the Gospel of John, some Psalms, and a few shorter passages. I offer dramatic presentations of these Scriptures from memory at women's retreats and other events, and then I speak on topics drawn from these passages.

When I memorize, I consider each word, each phrase, each action more carefully than I might by just reading the passage. The danger lies in encouraging others to live by these Scriptures without applying them to my own life. That would certainly mark me a Pharisee.

For instance, in John 12:1–11, which I've memorized, Mary pours out her precious ointment on the feet of Jesus. I love to share that Mary knew who Jesus was, knew what her treasure was, and didn't care what others thought. That leads me to consider what treasures I have in my closet that I might give to Jesus. If I'm not pouring my treasures out for Jesus, I am a Pharisee if I challenge others to do so.

Philippians 4:6–7 is a favorite verse: "Do not be anxious about anything, but in everything, by prayer and petition, with thanksgiving, present your requests to God. And the peace of God, which transcends all understanding, will guard your hearts and your minds in Christ Jesus." But living the truth of that verse is hard—because I'm a worrier.

For instance, right now I have physical problems involving my eyes and my ears. I have places to go and things to do. I don't have time to be sick. So I worry. And then I feel like a Pharisee. When I speak, I tell people they need not worry because God walks with them through every circumstance. I've memorized Psalm 139, which also reminds me that I can never get away from God's presence. So why am I anxious?

I am anxious because I don't want to become deaf or blind or, heaven forbid, both. I am anxious because my symptoms could indicate other disorders within my head.

It frightens me. To ward off worry, I look for what I can learn through the experience. For one thing, I can learn to be patient as doctors seek to understand my problem. After all, the apostle Paul "learned to be content" (Phil. 4:11). I can also learn to trust God (a thought from Proverbs 3:5–6, another memory passage). God has never ever let me down. He has seen me through one problem after another, a day at a time. So he won't desert me now. I remind myself of a phrase from a friend's blog: "Good will come from this." Instead of worrying, I ask God to work his wonders. I pray: "Lord, there is a problem. You know what it is, and I need your help to fix it. I remember and thank you for all the past times you've come to my aid, so I count on your grace to see me through this situation as well."

Instead of worrying, I concentrate on doing something for someone else. That gets my mind off my own problems. Right now my husband needs a major medical procedure. I will make him a favorite supper. I will encourage him instead of moping over my situation.

These actions move me from the realm of a Pharisee to the realm of a disciple, someone who is learning to walk with God, someone who is learning to work in partnership with him, regardless of thoughts and emotions. A disciple doesn't just memorize Scripture and talk about it.

—**Shirley Brosius**, author of *Sisterhood of Faith*